SPRING HILL, TENNESSEE

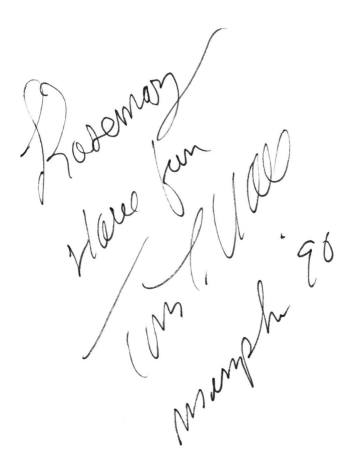

Rosemary
Have fun
[signature]
Memphis '90

SPRING HILL,

TENNESSEE

A Novel

TOM T. HALL

LONGSTREET PRESS
Atlanta, Georgia

Published by
LONGSTREET PRESS, INC.
2150 Newmarket Parkway
Suite 102
Marietta, Georgia 30067

Printed in the United States of America

Second Printing 1990

Library of Congress Catalog Card Number: 89:063796

ISBN 0-929264-73-8

This book was printed by R. R. Donnelley & Sons,
Harrisonburg, Virginia. The text was set in Caslon 540 by
Typo-Repro Service, Inc., Atlanta, Georgia. Design by
Laura Ellis. Cover illustration by Walt Floyd.

This book is dedicated to The Brotherhood, of whom there were, and are, many. To the few, and to my father, Reverend Virgil Lee Hall, who instilled in me a deep appreciation for the brotherhood of man and the responsibilities that go with it.

For
Will
Jim
Tom
Miller
Robert
Randy
John
Alex
Borden

What's good for the country is good for
General Motors, and vice versa.

> — Charles E. Wilson, former president of
> General Motors and Secretary of Defense,
> Eisenhower administration

CHAPTER ONE

GENESIS

Scott Zephries was often heard to say, "Show me a man who ain't got a sad history and I'll show you a man with a piss-poor memory."

He put an end to history as he knew it early one morning in February of 1958 in Spring Hill, Tennessee. He did it by shooting himself through the throat with a twelve-gauge, open choke shotgun while entangled in a barbed wire fence that surrounded his mother's farm. He was thought to be hunting at the time.

His mother, Amanda Zephries, got his insurance money. She had just recently been named the beneficiary.

Scott Zephries left two small sons — Phillip, one-and-a-half years, and Bill, two-and-a-half months old. Their mother, Rosanna Zephries, had left Scott Zephries's bed and board two weeks before. She had moved to Detroit, Michigan, in search of a good factory job that would bring her a prosperous and happy life away from Spring Hill, Tennessee. Amanda had been pleased to see what she had thought to be a difficult daughter-in-law leave the Old Zephries Place. She had managed to hide her delight from her distraught son.

With the death of Amanda Zephries's son and the absconding of her daughter-in-law, she was left with two small mouths to feed. She was saddened by her son's death, delighted at the mother's departure, and would not tempt her God by asking why any of it happened to be so.

As it was too cold and wet to plow in Tennessee in February of 1958, it was easy to find sufficient help to bury her son. He had wanted to be buried under the big oak tree at the rear of the house where his father, Gyp Zephries, lay at rest.

Amanda Zephries, her shawl wrapped about her shoulders, directed the digging of the grave. "He wants to be buried under that tree there. Why do you boys keep moving out there like that? He wants to be buried under that tree with his father."

The young black man who seemed to be in charge of the gravedigging said, "Ma'am, we can't dig in them roots. They too thick 'round there."

Amanda Zephries looked around in bewilderment. "Well, now, you can't put him there in my flower bed. You can't see now but in the spring and summer that's a nice flower bed. See all those rusty looking twigs? They'll be flowers in spring and summer and you can't put him there." The woman stared in confusion. "Oh, mercy. It's getting cold and it's getting late. Find a good soft spot here in this fencing and bury him there. Just get on with your work. Any place in here will do." Amanda returned to the house and banged the kitchen door behind her. She went immediately to the two-small boys, one in a cradle and one and in a crib. She said to her young black housekeeper, "Til, are these boys warm enough in here by this stove?"

"Uh huh, they all right there. You go on, I'se gonna watch 'em close."

The grandmother looked down at the sleeping children. "Lord, Lord, don't it beat anything? A mother who could leave two fine children like this? I know Scott had a crazy way, and he was no prize, but for a woman to leave two children as pretty as these is a mystery."

The tall, dark woman stood and stared at her grandchildren. She didn't want them to grow up to be bitter and vindictive, but she knew it would be a never ending job to keep them from being influenced by their circumstance and environment. She turned to Til and repeated, "A mystery, a real mystery."

Til said, "Like I done told you about my own daddy going off to the factories up north. He jus' jumped on a bus one Friday and never did come back. Broke my mama's heart and finally killed her. I know dat. Dat's why he named me Utility fo' he left. He said rich folks had utilities and he wanted me to grow up and have a name like rich folks could understand."

Amanda smoothed the children's blankets. She said, "Til, you have told that story a million times. Your name is not Utility, it's Til."

"Uh huh, but jus' in case my daddy come rollin' back dis way, I want somebody to know I's his daughter."

"Those boys are using our tools, so you make sure they put them back in the shed when they leave."

"Uh huh."

Preacher Joseph Armes wrestled his old car through the narrow turns of Sugar Ridge Road. He was on his way to pick up Amanda Zephries and escort her to the funeral home. The Old Zephries place came into view like a battered, weather-beaten old painting. Splotches of old white paint, a window here, a gable there, partially hidden behind huge oak and beech trees. Wild rose bushes lined the fence on the left, and weeds marched up toward the old two-story structure until they reached a mowed area that surrounded the circular drive. As the house became more visible, it was obvious that the old place had been built of substantial wood. There were no sagging corners or displacement of the roof. The house sat there stubbornly and regally among the aging trees and rolling countryside. A wide porch extended along the entire front of the house and mossy, pyramidal rock steps led to the porch and the heavy oak door that guarded the entrance hall. Six of the house's twelve rooms had been sealed off to conserve heat, including the huge formal dining room that had been the scene of festive parties in earlier years.

Amanda Zephries knelt by an old sofa in the front parlor. She began murmuring a prayer but stopped when she heard a car horn honk outside the front door. She called to the housekeeper in the kitchen, "Til, I'm going now to see how they have Scott laid out. I'll be back when I've finished."

"Uh huh."

"Now don't you get too close to that stove and fall asleep. You watch my babies."

"Uh huh."

Amanda Zephries stepped lightly through the thawing mud of her front yard. She wore black rubber boots covered by a long, dark skirt; her shawl was still wrapped around her shoulders. She spoke to the tall, stooped young preacher who held the door ajar on a blue '49 Chevrolet automobile. "Evening, Brother Joseph. How are you?"

"I'm fine, Mrs. Zephries."

As the car made its way down Sugar Ridge Road toward Spring Hill, Amanda Zephries spoke first. "Have you thought of something nice to say about my son, Preacher?"

"I've prayed about it."

"Well, it was an accident. You know that."

"The Lord knows if it was an accident."

4

"I suppose He does. The insurance company believes it was an accident. They're going to pay his insurance."

"That might make some difference. The Lord runs the biggest insurance company of them all."

Amanda did not turn her head, but she shifted her eyes toward the preacher and silently wished that he would refrain from being clever.

The pair rode silent.

Amanda could not guess why her son Scott had befriended this awkward young man who claimed to be a "called" preacher. She had often seen the two of them sitting on the tailgate of the old wagon that had rusted away down by the barn, and she had known that two young men could not talk so long about the weather.

Joseph Armes kept his free hand on the tattered black leather-bound Bible on the front seat of the car. It was his one source of comfort in life. Just inside the first plain pages of the book, under a heading of Births and Deaths, his father had written under births: Son, Joseph, May 17 1932, Maury County, Tennessee.

Joseph tugged at the loose collar and tie around his neck. It seemed that all of his clothes were ill-fitted to his slight frame. When he walked his pants legs flapped in the wind like a poorly pitched tent, and his coat could sometimes catch enough wind to actually blow him off line. He had grown so far out of the black pants that he was constantly tugging at his socks to hide his bare legs when he was sitting.

His father had also been a preacher. The senior Armes had made a living at horse and cattle trading, growing tobacco, and conducting weddings and funerals. He had turned an old abandoned schoolhouse into a church, although as Joseph remembered it, there were never more than eight or ten members. Joseph clearly recalled sitting outside on the wagon seat while his father shouted long fire-and-brimstone sermons.

It would be eight years after his father's death before the young Joseph would get the call. Both his parents had died in a flash flood, and their bodies had been brought out to the farmhouse for the funeral. It was on that day that he realized he did not know his parents' full names: Vernon Abel Armes and Opal Verona Armes. The man from the funeral home gave him the death certificates and the key to the big metal-bound trunk where the family's prize possessions were stored. He was seventeen years old at the time.

Joseph Armes went to a closet of the old house and found the black suit that his father had ordered from a church supply house. Although it did not fit so tall a man, it gave him a feeling of power and continuity. It was the suit that he wore on this evening with Amanda Zephries.

When the two mourners arrived at the funeral home, they found it was cold and poorly lighted. The funeral director, knowing that Mrs. Zephries was due to arrive, stood silently beside the open coffin of the late Scott Zephries. As the mother approached, the director made a few nervous moves to prepare for her inspection. He stepped aside. Amanda Zephries stood with her arms folded across her breasts. "He looks fine, he looks okay." She leaned closer to the body. "Why is the tie so far up under his chin? Can't you adjust the tie down some?"

The director squirmed and said, "Uh, well . . ." He looked at the preacher for help.

Brother Joseph said, "Amanda, he has a big hole in his neck."

The mother stood back a step and looked at the rest of the setting. There were a few flowers, some candles, a guest register, and some wooden chairs. She said, "Yes, of course he does. Of course."

She turned to the director and spoke in a businesslike manner. "It's done well, it's fine, thank you. Is there some place that Brother Joseph and I can talk in private?"

"Yes, of course. We have a small chapel off to the side here. I'm afraid it's not very warm in there."

"I don't want to pray. I just want to talk."

"Then you can use my office. There's a fire in there."

"Thank you."

Preacher Armes stirred the fire in the old coal-burning stove as Amanda Zephries seated herself. She was a big woman, near six feet tall. Her hair was black and cut medium short. She had large breasts and covered them modestly in a neck-high black wool sweater. She wore no jewelry. Her dark eyes took in the preacher as he finished stoking the coal fire and settled into a stiff-backed wooden chair. The woman spoke. "Scott got a letter from Rosanna."

"A letter?"

"Yes, it came a few days ago. I was debating showing it to him. He never saw it."

"That's too bad."

"Would you like to read it?"

"If you want me to."

The woman handed the blue envelope to the preacher. He brushed a strand of long brown hair from his eyes and began to read:

Detroit, Michigan
Feb. 58

Dear Scott,

This will be the hardest letter I have ever had to write. I want you to know that I love my children and pray that they will be okay.

I am here in Detroit and I am okay. I don't have an address

where you can write me yet. It is so cold here and I have not slept good since I left. I know it's cold in Spring Hill too.

The reason I left there and came here is not because I don't love you. I do. Your mother is the reason I left. We never should have moved in with her. You told me we would get a place of our own when the tobacco money came in and then you bought a new truck with the money. I waited almost two years for you to keep your promise.

Scott, I hate to say this, but it's the truth. I couldn't believe we could live in a place without indoor toilets. I was not raised that way. When my daddy found out where we were living he wanted me to come on back to Murfreesboro and live with him and mama. I should have done it I guess. You can't imagine a woman who is pregnant walking through the snow to get to the toilet. It broke my heart. I felt like a sow hog who was just having children because your mother wanted some. Between Amanda and Til I never could feel like Phillip was mine. And then little Bill came along and they took him over too.

Scott, it's hard for you to know what kind of woman your mother is. She can choke a person to death by just being in the same house with her. I guess it's that Louisiana French blood or something. I had to get out and I did. I am going to get a good job here and find a way to get my children back. I don't want to hurt you, but your mama has not heard the last of me. Well, you always said I talked and never did anything. Well, I've done something now and so I won't brag about it.

Scott, Til don't know it but she is a slave. Just as sure as she's born she is a slave. The law should do something. How can your mother keep that poor child out of school and there to do her every wish? If I could afford a lawyer some day I'll see to it that my children and Til are saved from that witch.

I know she's your mother, but this is true. Scott, don't go off drinking and brooding around about this. Just be brave and some day things will be okay. I know I can't get you or the kids from your mother right now so I won't even ask. You are caught in her trap. I'm sorry to say.

I have no doubt that Amanda will take care of what she calls her babies. But someday my children will know the truth.

When I get my job I'll send you some money for the boys. Be sure they get it and not Amanda. Well, what more can I say?

Love,
Rosanna

P.S. I left a little blue, velvet-covered box with some jewelry and trinkets in that chest of drawers in our room. Please give it to Til. She's the only decent thing that happened to me on that road, and I really want her to have it. Please do this for me if you do nothing else.

The preacher folded the letter and stared at the wall for a minute. He handed the letter back to Amanda Zephries without comment.

Amanda said, "I'm not sure I should have let you read this."

The young preacher seemed surprised. He stammered, "Uh, well . . . Now, I knew Scott Zephries as well as anybody. You don't have to hold anything back from me, Mrs. Zephries."

The dark woman's eyes glistened. She leaned forward, opened the door of the stove and dropped the blue envelope into the flames.

The preacher closed the door of the stove. He placed the palms of his hands together as if to pray and spoke in a soft voice. "Mrs. Zephries, this funeral has begun. You do not fully realize it yet, but your son is dead. There are many things to be buried."

The two sat silent for a moment. The preacher raised his head toward the ceiling; his eyes caught a cobweb covered with soot. He coughed and mumbled, "It ought to be against the law to burn coal inside a house."

The ride back to Sugar Ridge was cold. The car's engine had cooled, and the heater was slow in responding to the night's air. The young preacher drove slowly down state road 31 North and turned left on Depot Street.

Amanda Zephries's thoughts were far away. She wrapped her shawl tighter around her shoulders and remembered the first time she had journeyed to the ridge. It was in the spring of 1931 when she was seventeen years of age. Her aunt and uncle had sent her north to Spring Hill, Tennessee, with forty-seven-year-old Harlan "Gyp" Zephries. Amanda had lived a closely guarded and managed life with her Aunt and Uncle Thibodaux, and so they had also arranged her marriage. It was on the long train ride from New Orleans in a stateroom that the union was consummated. Her parents, like Gyp Zephries's wife and children, had died in the great influenza epidemic of the year 1919. She had not argued with the arrangement of her marriage to the well-mannered, well-dressed mule trader and world traveler. He had said, "The influenza has separated us from the ones we loved and in doing so has brought us together. So be it."

She bore him two sons — Nathaniel Banks Zephries, killed in the Korean War in 1953, and Scott, now lying dead in the funeral home.

Gyp Zephries had died a violent death when he was shot and killed over a mule trading deal at the old Thompson's Station Bucket Factory.

Now Amanda Zephries was once again left to raise two small children. She started to remark to the preacher that she was getting a new lease on life at the age of forty-four but thought better of it. Her Louisiana French ancestors had a phrase for it: *C'est la vie.*

The preacher turned on the car radio. Elvis Presley was singing "You Ain't Nothing But A Hound Dog"; the preacher quickly flipped it off. Amanda wrapped her shawl more tightly around her shoulders like a tourniquet, as if doing so would shut off the flow of memories. She said, "I can't stand that music."

The preacher mumbled, "I was looking for the news. Harry Truman says Eisenhower is leading us into another depression."

The two didn't speak during the remainder of the ride to Sugar Ridge. The woman laid her head back on the seat and closed her eyes. The memories returned.

Amanda Zephries had an idyllic notion of her childhood. She thought she could remember a perfect peace. There were summer days with the sound of horses clomping up in front of her uncle's grocery store. She loved the snorting of the horses and the sun rays that filtered through the dust from the well-traveled dirt road that ran in front of the store. She could distinctly remember the brightly colored signs nailed onto the front and sides of the weathered old building that was the center of her universe when she was a child. Not knowing that the signs were advertisements, she thought of them as decoration.

As a slim, dark child, she had come to live with her aunt and uncle, Mary and Peter Thibodaux, after her parents had died. She was five at the time.

In later years, when she would be hungry, she would remember the smell of Cajun food cooking. When she was depressed she would remember the laughter and music of her childhood. And when she was lonely she could recall the fondness that the visitors to her uncle's grocery store had had for her. She had been the only child on the premises, since Pete and Mary Thibodaux's children were grown. At the store she was often referred to as Princess, Queenie, and Movie Girl. No endearment seemed too extravagant.

Amanda grew up well-to-do by local standards. Her education at public schools and by private tutors had been exceptional. She was encouraged to strive for excellence in her schooling and was scolded for speaking the local dialect of Acadian French. Her aunt would often say, "By the time you are a teenage, I won you to spoke Englis good. No?" Her aunt Mary instilled in her a general distrust of men. Amanda was taught to tolerate but not to encourage the dominating males of Chalmette, Louisiana, a stone's throw from New Orleans. She could remember eyeing the young men who came to the store and wondering how such mean creatures as her aunt described could be housed in such charming young bodies. Her aunt was a strict disciplinarian who gave stark and honest lectures about sex, whiskey, and sin. The naive and artless, but honest, lectures left her with few sexual misconceptions. She was a well-suited and well-trained wife for the adventurous and cosmopolitan Gyp Zephries. She was also a bitter and disappointed adult who subconsciously missed the worship she had enjoyed as a child.

The day they had brought her husband Gyp Zephries home in the back of a wagon, explaining that he had been killed in a "fair" fight, Amanda had been shocked into a realization of a justice of her own definition. She had lost her fear of God on that day. And the day the telegram arrived telling her that her son Nat had been "killed in action," the already hard-eyed woman took a steely view of life and decided to manage it on her own terms. For a long while she would succeed handsomely.

When the preacher dropped the widow back at the Old Zephries Place, Til met her at the door. Til's large, questioning eyes glistened from a flat face. "Lawd, you looks awful. You let me fix you a julep."

"No, I don't think . . . oh, well, just a small one, Til. And don't warm the water, it'll put me to sleep. I have some things to do."

"You needs to be relaxin' yo'self some now. Dey be pullin' at you all day tomorrow."

"Did they finish the grave?" Amanda Zephries peered through the glass in the kitchen window into the back of the property.

"Uh huh, they did a real good job on it. They wanted me to pay 'em. I say, Lawd, I ain't got no kinda money. They say they come back tomorrow early. It's six dollars apiece."

"Don't worry about it. Have my babies been asleep?"

"Uh huh, they sleep like little kittens. I changed the little 'un. Fixed him a bottle. Dat big ornery boy put his legs up on de side of de crib and was sleepin' with his legs stuck up in de air. I move him around."

The housekeeper busied herself with the julep as she talked. She put a tablespoon of sugar into a glass of water, stirred in an ounce of bourbon whiskey, and added a small piece of peppermint candy to the glass. She set the glass in front of her mistress and suddenly burst into tears. "Oh, Lawd, Lawd, my poor Scotty, blessed little boy of God. Bless his heart. Bless his heart."

Amanda Zephries rose quickly, placed her hands on the shoulders of the black girl, and began to shake her as she spoke in quietly excited tones. "Til, stop it! You'll wake the children. Stop it! There'll be time for that."

The girl continued to weep and wail. "Lawd, blessed Jesus. Poor Scotty. He was a fine boy, Lawd. A mighty fine young man dat you took into yo' precious fold."

Amanda steered the girl toward the back of the house, still admonishing her in a strong, quiet voice. "Go to your room,

Til. If you can't control yourself, go to your room!"

Til Jefferson, only seventeen years old, fell across the bed in her small room and mourned the loss of Scott Zephries in the only way she knew. She cried, and she moaned and repeated the name, "Poor little Scotty, poor little Scotty. Lawd, Lawd."

Til's folks had moved to Spring Hill in 1938 when State Road 31 had been paved. It was good work that the girl's father had enjoyed in building the road. But the road seemed to take more from Maury County than it brought. Work declined and the father moved away to Michigan in search of a factory job that lured so many young people away from Middle Tennessee. When her mother died, Til was alone in the world. Amanda Zephries learned of the young girl's plight through the church and brought her to the Old Zephries Place as a gesture of charity. Sherman Cooper, a Nashville attorney and family friend, secured a letter of guardianship from Til's father in Michigan. Amanda Zephries quickly removed the young girl from the influence of the black community by proclaiming that she would be educated at home. Til Jefferson was taught to read and write, laboriously tutored in basic math, and there her formal education ended. Amanda, the matron of the Old Zephries Place, said the girl was not educationally inclined.

The morning of the funeral dawned gray. The usual sound of a fire being built in the kitchen stove roused Amanda Zephries from her troubled sleep.

The two young boys slept in the housekeeper's room where a small electric heater kept them warm through the nights. Til Jefferson kept vigil in her single bed, a few feet away from the children.

As it was every morning at the Old Zephries Place, the lady of the house waited until she could smell coffee brewing before rising to her morning constitution. She dressed quickly in clothes that she had laid out the night before, left her room and went down the winding staircase to the parlor, turned left toward the kitchen, murmured a good morning to the young black girl, inquired about "her babies," and exited the kitchen door to make the short walk to the toilet a few yards from the rear of the house.

As she walked toward the outhouse, Amanda saw the grave-site of her son. The raw black earth at the sides of the grave had been laid over with artificial grass. Frost glistened on the bright green surface as the first rays of sunlight skipped across the old farm.

From the kitchen window, the young housekeeper watched as the woman knelt in the cold, dormant grass and offered a prayer.

The girl turned from the window and mumbled to herself. "Dat woman mighty firm a mind. One minute she fightin' de Lawd, next minute she talkin' to him."

Amanda returned to the house and sat at the kitchen table drinking coffee. The housekeeper put the woman's breakfast in front of her. "Hope you feeling okay today; yo' babies is fine. They slept good most of the night," the girl said.

The older woman looked appraisingly at the young black girl. "What are you doing in that garb this morning?"

Til pretended to take sudden note of what she was wearing. She looked down at her black, high-heeled shoes, nylon hose, black satin dress, and white cotton jacket. She spoke defiantly, "Dis ain't no garb, dis is my funeral clothes."

"You're not going to a funeral. The funeral is coming here."

Til put her hand over her mouth and said, "Why they not having no regular funeral? Why dat crazy man preachin' de funeral anyway?" She always placed her hand over her mouth and talked in muffled tones when she suspected that she was out of place.

Amanda said, "Get your hand out of your mouth. Lord, I don't know how Scott ever got to know this strange young preacher. He was down on the street corner preaching one Saturday morning, and Scott walked right up to him and invited him up here for lunch. At first, Brother Joseph scared me to death. He actually foams at the mouth when he gets to preaching on the street. But when he got here he was just as polite as you please and never mentioned the Bible, his religion or anything about the church."

Til interrupted. "He could haint a house in dat suit he got."

Amanda continued as if she didn't hear her. "He was the only preacher Scott ever knew, and when he came by here after the accident I couldn't turn him down for the funeral. He doesn't have a church that I know of. You know, Til, in the old days we always had funerals at home. I don't remember when they started laying the body out in a funeral home or a church." Amanda Zephries stopped talking and looked around the room as if she had just awakened from a short sleep. She patted her hair into place and groaned, "Oh, well, it's all the same here or there or whatever. It won't be a long service."

"Well, jus' the same, I'se gonna look nice when Mister Scotty come home."

Amanda shrugged in resignation. "Well, for God's sake, don't wear that white jacket. Get something dark. White is not appropriate."

"Mister Scotty liked dis jacket. White folks don't know how to dress fo' funerals no way."

Amanda decided that she could not win an argument with the girl under such circumstances. She walked to the kitchen window and looked outside. Holding the coffee cup in her hand and staring into the brown liquid, she spoke determinedly. "Til, you know what I'm going to do with Scott's insurance money? I'm going to have a bathroom put into this house.

Two of them. One for you and the boys and one for me, upstairs."

The black girl said, "It's bad luck to make plans on a funeral day."

"Who told you that?"

"It ain't nothin' nobody told me. It's a fact."

A young man from the funeral home knocked gently on the front door of the Old Zephries Place. Til answered the knock and admitted the young man who had brought some wooden folding chairs to place in the parlor of the house. Til moved a few small pieces of furniture to help the man clear a place for the casket to be displayed.

They placed it on a rack and the funeral director prepared the body for viewing. The once large parlor looked small now, with the chairs all along the middle and sides and the casket taking up the space between the windows of the high ceiling room. As the mourners began to arrive and find seats, the floors creaked with the unaccustomed weight. The funeral home had provided a small table on which rested a guest register lighted by a horizontal, shaded light. A record player hidden somewhere behind the racks of flowers that surrounded the casket played solo organ renditions of familiar church hymns.

Til Jefferson, who had never hosted a social affair at the Old Zephries Place, found herself in charge for a few minutes. Amanda had gone upstairs to refresh herself, and Til stood at the door that led from the parlor to the kitchen and whispered "uh huh's" and "naw naw's" to the guests and the funeral director. With inward disapproval, she watched the crowd gather. Presently she heard Amanda come down the stairs and watched her make her way to the front of the room, where she shook a few hands and accepted condolences from those in attendance.

Preacher Joseph Armes stepped to the front and commanded the small space between the casket and the first row of chairs. He had a small notebook tucked into his hand beneath his battered old black Bible. He stood there for a moment seeming to search for notes, cleared his throat, looked about him uncomfortably, then moved to the end of the casket and stepped back beside it. He asked for bowed heads and a prayer. "Lord, Almighty God, Creator of the universe, Heavenly Father. These mourners come to Thee with heavy hearts today. They come to Thee with a new knowledge, a new understanding. For they now know that life here on this earth is indeed short. That their time on this earth is meaningless in the grand scheme of things. We ask Thee to give them courage this day to bear up under the burdens they face in losing a dear friend and family member. Be with them, Lord, now, in this hour of need. We ask it in Jesus's name, amen."

Amanda knew that it was not unusual for a preacher to proselytize for more than an hour at funerals. She had attended funerals where much weeping, crying, and fainting had gone on, making the solemn event seem more a camp meeting or revival than a burial. There would be none of that on this day. Amanda Zephries caught the tone of the opening prayer and looked directly at the face of Joseph Armes as he thumbed through his notes. Her stare held the perspiring brow of the preacher until his head lifted and he looked at her. She stared deep into his eyes and left the message that she would not tolerate a long harangue on fire and brimstone.

Joseph Armes looked into the dead face of Scott Zephries. He remembered the confused young man when he was alive. He remembered the arguments he had had with the young farmer. Scott Zephries had said, "If there's a God like you say, he sure ain't showed his face around here for a long time."

Joseph Armes said, "What do you mean by a long time?"

"Well, say a hundred years."

"A day is the same as a hundred years in the eyes of God."

Scott Zephries laughed. "Where do you guys learn to talk like that? Is there a school that teaches you to answer every question in the world with a Bible quotation?"

The preacher started to quote more scripture but thought better of it. He said, "The Bible is a source of inspiration and information."

"Does God know what's going to happen tomorrow?"

"God gave us free will. We can do what we will with tomorrow, according to His will."

"Does God know if I'll be alive next week?"

"Why shouldn't you be alive next week?"

Scott Zephries stared off into the distant clouds and said, "What if I exercised my free will?"

Joseph was jarred back to the present by a hand on his shoulder. The undertaker said, "We should continue."

The lanky preacher reflected for a moment on what Scott Zephries had said that day just more than a week ago. He had not known what to make of the question at the time; he understood now.

The preacher was sweating about the collar of his starched white shirt. He was torn between the visual instructions Amanda Zephries had given him and the higher notion of his evangelical calling.

The twenty-six-year-old preacher wanted desperately to please Amanda Zephries. He expected a handsome donation for his work after the services, and he needed the social favors of widow Zephries. He had long known her to be one of the most influential women in all of Maury County. But he also believed that he could preach a suicide into heaven. Reverend Armes had thought about it on several occasions and had always wanted to preach a suicide. He entertained the notion that it was the devil who pulled the trigger on such deaths, it was Satan who put the pills in the mouths of the overdosers, and it was the devil who pushed people from the bridges and buildings where they fell to their deaths.

Now he stood torn between two great passions — preaching and professionalism. Scott Zephries had once told him, "It's okay to have ambitions, but first you gotta get elected." With that in mind, Joseph Armes read meekly from a few snatches of scripture, murmured another short prayer, and asked that the bereaved retire to the grave site at the rear of the house.

Amanda and Til waited by the kitchen door. The two women stood restlessly as the small events of the ceremony went on about them. The casket was brought out the front door and around the house to the back; the flower racks were carried around to the grave site. It was done quickly and in whispered voices. A shiver went through the body of Amanda Zephries, and Til grabbed the tall woman's arm with one hand and patted the arm with the other. Then the two ladies seated themselves on the chairs provided for them.

Preacher Armes stood silent as the casket was placed over the grave. He motioned the pallbearers to stand aside and started to read and speak again.

Rosanna Zephries, wife of the deceased, stood before a receptionist's desk at an employment agency in Detroit, Michigan. The receptionist referred to a note on her desk, looked up at the hopeful young woman and said, "I think you've got the job. Doctor Atworth says you'll do just fine."

When the funeral was over, two young men who had been pallbearers sat in the cab of their pickup truck smoking cigarettes and passing a small bottle of whiskey between them. One said, "You know, I been thinking about that grave. Ain't that right where we moved that outhouse from last summer? I mean, we moved it about twenty feet and dug a new hole and helped him drag that two-holer over there where it is now. Didn't we?"

The other boy laughed and took a drink from the bottle of whiskey. "I swear, I think old Scott was the unluckiest son of a bitch I ever met. He married a beautiful broad and she left him, shot hisself with his best bird gun, and now they buried him in a shithole."

Til Jefferson checked on the children, noted that Amanda Zephries had gone upstairs, wrapped the discarded black shawl about her, and went out back to pay the two black men who were filling the grave with dirt. She handed them six dollars each and stood looking at the grave. One of the young men spoke. "It's cold, ain't it?"

The girl said, "It's sposed to be cold dis time a year."

"We see you in church. You sing mighty good."

"I see you too."

"You ever need a ride to church?"

"What would I need a ride fo'? I rides with de boss lady. She drop me off at my church and she go to hers and then she pick me up and we come right back here. What fo' would I need no ride, I'd like to know?"

The young man dropped his head in face of this logic. "You must have some kinda fun going to church with a old white lady."

"I don't go to church fo' fun. I go to praise de Lawd."

There was sudden clatter from the upstairs of the old house. All heads turned toward the noise of crying and crashing of furniture.

Til Jefferson said in a sighing voice, "Well, I reckon she turning loose now dat it's all over. Lawd, dat woman is firm a mind."

CHAPTER TWO

JUST LIKE OLD TIMES

(Twenty-seven years later)

Amanda Zephries hollered from her chair on the front porch, "Til, remind me again not to tell Phillip about my headaches when he gets here. I get to rambling on and then he'll think I'm sick and he'll get on to me about not writing and telling him about it."

Til Jefferson came onto the porch and sat down in one of the old wicker rocking chairs. She folded her apron in her lap and smiled as she spoke. "I swear, I think I'll faint when I see dat boy. I'se also gonna knock him down if he come in here all college talking and smarty like he is sometimes. Would you ever believe dat our little Phillip is almost thirty years old and gone off in the world? I swear, it seems like nothing ever change around here 'cept people coming and going."

Amanda waved away a bee that buzzed the porch. She looked off down the road as she spoke. "Can't you get Bill to get up now?"

"Naw, he up there in bed with dat hussy from Columbia. I swear, I don't see why you put up with dat kind of goin's on."

"Til, I think it's my fault. It's the Cajun blood in him. If we tell him he can't do something here, he'd go do it some-place else. Just leave him alone and maybe he'll grow out of it."

Til rocked faster. "Can't you hear 'em up there gruntin' and groanin'? I'd say a man oughta have more respect for his Grandma den dat. All time drankin' and rootin' 'round."

"Well, Phillip's plane doesn't get in until four-thirty. They'll surely be up by that time."

"If they ain't, I gonna throw a bucket of water on 'em." Both women laughed at the prospect.

Sally Weeds sat on the side of the bed and stared at the sleeping form of Bill Zephries. She whispered, "Bill, you awake? Bill!"

The tall, dark man in the bed raised up and ran his fingers through his hair. "Well, if I was asleep, I ain't now. What time is it?"

Sally looked at her watch. "One-thirty."

"Holy shit. Phillip's coming in from St. Louis this afternoon."

Bill Zephries, the youngest of Amanda Zephries's "babies," had taken to the farm at an early age. He graduated from the old Spring Hill High School that had been built in 1937, borrowed money to buy some new farm equipment, bought up several nice tobacco allotments, and now raised the profitable crop on a full-time basis. His free time was spent hunting, fishing, chasing women and drinking beer. In Spring Hill, Tennessee, in the year 1985, Bill Zephries was envied, if not respected.

The attractive blonde woman pushed Bill back onto the bed. She laid her head on his chest and whispered, "Bill? Tell me again what you're gonna get me when you sell this place."

"A Jeep. I told you a hundred times. A Jeep."

"Well, now, don't get mad. I just like to hear you say it. I'm gonna take the top off, and the doors off, and go anywhere I please."

"Well, you ain't going too far in a Jeep with the top off and the doors off in the middle of winter."

The girl stretched on the side of the bed and reached for her underclothes. "You reckon Phillip will want to sell?"

"I don't know what he's thinkin'." Bill shook the sleep from his eyes. "But we're selling. Anybody with a college education should be able to figure out that three million dollars is a lot of money." He sat up on the side of the bed and reached for a cigarette.

Sally said, "What are you gonna do with Amanda and Til? They don't want to leave."

"Aw, they can live anywhere they please. We got three hundred acres of prime real estate here in the back door of the world's biggest auto plant."

"Bill, how much does a Jeep cost?"

"Sally, I don't know. Let's get first things first. Okay?"

Sally Weeds lay on the bed and listened to the shower running. She stuck her bare toes to the light by the window and examined her nails. She caught her reflection in the mirror and was pleased to see she still had her cheerleader figure. She sat up on the side of the bed and looked out the window into the tops of the tall trees that surrounded the Old Zephries Place. She loved the fall of the year, before it became cold and muddy. Her fondest memories were of her time as a cheerleader for the Spring Hill Raiders football team. She had had real friendships, real laughter, real excitement in competition, and a real life. It was after high school when she had married Gorman Weeds that things had gone wrong. Gorman was a bad man with bad habits and unpredictable meanness. He had beaten her more than once.

She stayed near Bill Zephries for more reasons than one. Bill was her guardian as well as her lover and provider. If it had not been for Bill Zephries, she was sure that she would have had to leave Maury County. Gorman Weeds was not a man so foolish as to mess with the farmer.

Sally picked up an old football that Bill kept in the room. A cheer ran though her head as she held the ball. She walked to the window and raised it slightly to smell the fall air. Her mind turned to her parents who were now separated and remarried. It had all happened so suddenly while she was married to Gorman. Sally was working in a Nashville night club at the time. She never really got all of the story, but her parents had encountered one another in a restaurant, her mother with a boyfriend and her father with a girlfriend. There had been three silent days before both of them started quietly packing to move out of the house where Sally was born and raised. She often wondered about the quiet guilt that must have hovered over that household for those three short days. What could be said?

Her father had gone south and her mother had gone north, and she sometimes got cards from them on special days. But for the most part she felt as though she were an orphan, or at least abandoned.

Sally Weeds shook the past from her head and gathered her overnight bag from the floor. She rummaged through it for her fingernail polish and held her nails to the light of the window. As she applied the polish she glanced at a newspaper Bill had dropped to the floor at the side of the bed. A pair of jeans covered part of the newspaper; she moved them with her foot and read more about the event that had changed the lives of almost everyone in Spring Hill.

A few weeks before, General Motors had announced that Spring Hill was to be the site of a new three-and-a-half billion dollar automobile plant called Saturn. There had been some reports that the plant might be located in Tennessee, but the thought that it would come to a little town of eleven hundred astounded most people.

There had been an absolute explosion of speculation in real estate. The people of Spring Hill had gone to bed in a quiet country village and had awakened to the news that they now lived in an industrial hot spot.

Sally's mind wandered to the recent and frequently told story of the firewood salesman. He had been a young country boy who cut firewood with a chainsaw during the week and sold it from the back of an old pickup in supermarket parking lots on weekends. When the real estate boom hit, the young man had sold his farm, bought a new Lincoln Continental, and left town. He had stopped long enough to throw two perfectly good chain saws into the Duck river.

Sally heard the hum of Bill's electric razor. She smiled to herself and felt a thrill of excitement in knowing that her boyfriend in the bathroom was soon to be a millionaire. She had always dreamed of having her own cocktail lounge, and Bill had always planned on someday building a big, modern tobacco warehouse in Spring Hill. With the arrival of Saturn, maybe all of their dreams would come true.

She stood and looked out the window, waving her fingers in the air to dry the polish, and vowed to hang onto this lover at all costs.

Bill came out of the bathroom and started pulling on jeans and a T-shirt. He flipped the towel at Sally's backside as she stood by the window. "See you downstairs," he said.

Sally could hear the old stairs creaking as the carefree young man took them two at a time on the way down to the kitchen where coffee was still brewing.

On the front porch, Til and Amanda continued to rock and talk. Amanda said, "You know, Til, if I had known that this Saturn Plant was even a notion in anybody's head, I'm not sure I would have deeded this place over to my grandchildren. I have managed the estate of the late Harlan Zephries pretty well. It seems a shame that after all these years of wise investment and management someone should throw a thing like this in my path. I suppose it's the price we pay. I was trying to avoid those inheritance taxes. Now I am at the mercy of the judgment of my grandchildren. I know Sherman Cooper meant well. Who in Spring Hill would have ever dreamed of such a thing as Saturn!"

"Dey'll listen to you. You wait and see."

Amanda Zephries frowned. "Ah, Bill won't. He says sell, sell, sell. I guess if I were his age, I'd feel the same way about it. I'm just too old to travel, Til."

"You ain't too old for nothin'. When Phillip gets here, you set them boys down and say your piece. I say dey'll listen."

Phillip Zephries wiped his glasses on his necktie and peered through the window of TWA flight 427. He caught sight of Old Hickory Lake shimmering in the bright November afternoon sunshine and felt a chill run down his back.

He did not like the notion of coming back to Spring Hill. His mind and spirit resented the backwoods nature of his childhood. His studies at Middle Tennessee State University had broadened his interests and widened his knowledge of the world. He told his friends and coworkers in St. Louis that he was from Nashville. The lie seemed easier than trying to explain where Spring Hill was located.

Phillip Zephries was a trim, dark-haired young man who could have passed for his brother Bill, except for his glasses and the notable difference in dress and speech. He was a half-inch shorter than his brother at 6'1", and was a little trimmer as a matter of difference in lifestyles. Bill had always been the one for fast foods and beer. Phillip had been pampered by his grandmother and Til and had developed a natural dread of too much food. He could still see the two guardians standing over him coaxing him to eat more. Football had been a similar experience with the coach always urging players to put some meat on their bones.

Phillip had enjoyed football for a lot of reasons. It got him out of the classroom, it gave him a chance to get out of Spring Hill once in a while, and nothing in the curriculum could beat football as a booster for the ego. Phillip had been a good player, and as the quarterback he had learned to think on his feet. It was something not everybody could do. But as comfortable as he was on the football field, he was equally uncomfortable with women.

Growing up in a home without young girls around had always caused Phillip to believe that there was something mysterious about women. He did not understand their moods and motivations, so he avoided close association with them. He had grappled with the problem at Spring Hill and later at college in Murfreesboro. He had given considerable thought to his bachelorhood. He had an underlying fear of being thought effeminate, and yet he could not, or had not, found that woman he wanted to spend the rest of his life with.

His brother Bill was a different kind of man. Bill said that women are women, men are men, and thank God for that little bit of difference. Phillip smiled as he thought of his brother that he would soon see. Bill was a horse trader who would strike up any kind of a deal for any profitable reason. Bill had a reputation in Spring Hill as a wheeler-dealer, part-time everything, seasonal tobacco farmer, and ladies' man. It was a reputation not unlike the one his grandfather Gyp Zephries had left him as a legacy. If Bill had dressed in his grandfather's clothes and worn a mustache, there would have been a striking resemblance in the man and grandson. Bill Zephries was a walking manifestation of an often expressed maxim: The apples do not fall far from the tree.

Now, as the plane landed at the Nashville Municipal Airport, Phillip set his jaw firm and decided to get out of Spring Hill and his past as soon as possible. He would dispense with this real estate business and be back in St. Louis in a few days. He rented a compact car, threw his small amount of luggage in the trunk, took I-65 south to the Franklin exit, drove out past the Williamson County Hospital, and picked up Carter's Creek Pike.

He drove leisurely past the big farms and grazing cattle. The leaves were turning colors on the trees. The old creek was occasionally visible from the road, and he thought of the many days of his childhood when he had found adventure and excitement in the creek just wading or fishing. He thought of changing values and the price of real estate.

Amanda, Til, Sally Weeds, and Bill Zephries were all sitting on the front porch when Phillip surprised them by coming in the back way to the Old Zephries Place. He walked through the kitchen door and yelled, "Hey! Anybody home around here?"

Til was first on her feet. She jumped up and swung the front door wide. "What you doin' sneakin' up on folks? You 'fraid somebody see you visitin' poor relatives? Get yo'self on out here and let us look at you."

Bill, who was sitting on the edge of the porch with Sally, said, "Grab a beer and shake some dust off your butt. You dodgin' the law, coming in the back roads?" He smiled broadly.

Phillip said, "Just wanted to see the country."

Amanda Zephries stood and held the young Phillip in a long embrace. Then she held him at arms length and said, "Phillip, oh, Phillip, you are so handsome. And so welcome."

Bill got to his feet and shook hands with his brother. "Phillip, this here's Sally Weeds. You remember her. She was cheerleading when you and them Wildcats took the championship."

Phillip shook hands with the girl and for an instant considered the shape of her body. She wore jeans, a T-shirt, and a pair of red leather shoes. Her hair was windblown and her movements were casual and relaxed. He thought of all the women in St. Louis who worked at dieting, exercising, and makeup and never looked this good. He imagined this woman on a diet of cheeseburgers and beer and marveled at the phenomenal trick nature played on some women. He spoke foolishly, recalling one of the high school cheers. "Hi there, Sally. I'm your man. If I can't do it, nobody can."

Sally Weeds smiled and said, "Hi. Welcome home."

Phillip turned quickly to his grandmother. "Well, Amanda, am I in for a country dinner, or are we eating at the Poplar House?"

Amanda motioned to Til. "This woman has been cooking for three days, knowing you were coming."

Bill said, "I'll get your bags out of the car. Keys in it?"

"Yes. In the ignition."

"Come on, Sally. Make yourself useful."

The two lovers went into the house as Til excused herself to check on something in the oven. Phillip took one of the rockers and stretched his arms above his head in the warm afternoon. "Well, Amanda, tell me all about it."

31

Amanda Zephries yelled into the house, "Til, bring us some coffee, please!"

From within the house, "Uh huh."

The woman leaned forward and clasped her hands together. "Lord, it's been a madhouse here in this little town. Til and I went out and stuck up a 'Not For Sale' sign one day. Bill took it down, but I swear they were tramping all over the place looking for land to buy. It's cooled off some. I don't see any way to keep from selling. Bill is all for it. Says we're millionaires sitting around like wooden Indians. What have you thought about it?"

"I read the papers and saw it on TV all the way in St. Louis. I didn't envy your having to deal with them. What was the best offer?"

"Nothing in writing. But everybody says nearly three million."

Phillip whistled. "That's a lot of money."

Amanda sat upright in her chair. "That is what it's all about, isn't it? A lot of money. We can't seem to get past the money. It's as if they can buy anything. Anything."

"Money talks."

"And I resent that so much."

The two sat silent for a minute, looking off down the road where the red and yellow leaves shimmered in the afternoon sun. They each remembered the road for different reasons: Phillip for the times he had run and played there; Amanda for the times she had looked lovingly at the old house as she returned from some short trip.

Amanda spoke. "You know, this house seems small now. But when your grandfather first brought me here those many years ago, it looked like a castle. It was one of the biggest houses in Maury County."

"Do you suppose they intend to pave the whole county?"

"There will soon be four hundred contractors moving in here. Where do you suppose they intend to put them? How many people is that?"

Bill and Sally came onto the porch. Bill said, "I put your things in your room. Let's go down to the Hitch Inn Post and have a beer before dinner. I'll show you around a little."

Amanda said, "Now, Bill, he just got home and you want to drag him off to a beer joint. Let the boy rest."

Phillip said, "I think I'd like to look around a little before it gets dark. We'll be back in a few minutes, Amanda. I promise."

Bill jangled the truck keys in his hand. "Hope you don't mind riding in a pickup. The Mercedes is out being polished." He laughed and then said, "I'll bring the truck around. We'll drop Sally by her place on the way in."

Amanda Zephries and Til Jefferson stood on the porch and waved as the pickup rolled out of the drive and onto Sugar Ridge Road. Til said, wiping her hands on her apron, "It's good to have them boys back together again. Like old times."

"Yes, it is good. But this time they're not talking hunting, fishing, and football."

CHAPTER THREE

THE DEAL

The pickup made old familiar noises as it bounced down Sugar Ridge Road. Phillip rode with his arm hanging over the side of the open window; Sally Weeds rode in the middle and Bill drove.

The trees that lined the roads in Spring Hill were oak, poplar, ash, hickory, walnut, beech, elm, sugar tree, and an occasional scrub oak, trees that had been there when Stephen D. Lee's Corps and Chalmer's Cavalry held off attacks by Wood's Fourth Corps and Wilson's Calvary in 1864 in the Civil War. Before the war the Eastern part of the county was a mass of cedar forest. Many of those trees had been used for rails, fence posts, shingles, and logs for houses. Later in the history of Maury County, this same forest was used for telegraph posts and by local pencil factories for lead pencils.

Phillip was very aware that Sally Weeds's hand lay casually on his knee. He shrugged his shoulders and moved closer to the window. Sally said, "I'd kinda like a beer myself, Bill."

Bill Zephries jerked the wheel of the pickup to the left and turned on to Beechcroft Road. "Naw, I'm gonna drop you off at your trailer. Me and Phillip got some catching up to do here. We ain't seen each other in a month of Sundays. Right, Phillip?"

"That's right."

Sally folded her arms across her considerable breasts. "You promised to take me over to Nashville to eat at the Cajun's Wharf one night this week."

Bill put his arm around her. "Well, now you ain't plannin' on dying tonight are you? There's other days comin' down the road, darlin'; big time days, if you ask me."

Phillip sat silent, slightly embarrassed by his brother's direct manner. Bill stopped the pickup in front of Sally's trailer. He opened his side of the vehicle and got out, reaching a hand for the woman. "Hey, keep your door shut and your pants on, honey. I'll be checkin' on you tomorrow," he said.

Once outside the truck, the woman put her hands on her hips. "What am I supposed to do all night?"

"Do what I told you. Just do what old Bill says, honey."

Bill swung the truck off Beechcroft onto Route 31, past Fox's Barber Shop, the Co-op, and the Poplar House Restaurant and out toward the Hitch Inn Post.

When his eye caught the Budwieser and Coors beer signs, it also caught something else. He spun the truck around in the parking area in front of the Hitch Inn Post and headed back toward Spring Hill. Dust covered the truck for a few seconds. Caught by surprise, Phillip slid to the floorboard of the truck and yelled, "What! What the hell was that?"

Bill straightened himself and the truck and laughed. "Bad company in that joint tonight. Bad company."

"Who is it?"

"Sally's old man is in there with Muff and Puff."

Phillip had collected himself. "You mean Muff and Puff are still running together?"

"Yeah, I think they were over-coached when they played football with you. I think it's okay to be twins, but these guys have hung out since they were kids. And they take sides with Gorman Weeds just to piss me off. Sally was married to Gorman for a while. They lived over in Columbia. She wanted to come back over here with me and it pissed Gorman off. They're divorced, but he won't let go."

"Doesn't that bother you?"

"Well, yes, it bothers me. I've had to kick his ass twice already, and one of these days I'm gonna have to hurt him if he don't learn some manners."

"Good God, this town will never change, will it?"

Bill laughed and patted his brother on the back. "Oh yeah, it's fixin' to change pretty soon now. You oughta stick around for some of the fun."

Bill bought a six-pack of Coors beer at Kirk's Bi-Rite and drove south to Neapolis Roadside Park. He drove the truck off the pavement and down the slope toward the two old wooden outside toilets. He opened his door, and hung his long legs across the window of the pickup. He opened two of the beers and handed one to Phillip. "You know somethin', little brother? We're rich. Did you ever expect to be rich?"

Phillip got out of the truck, closed the door, and leaned his arms on the open window, looking into the truck at his brother.

"We've always been rich, in a philosophical sense."

Bill turned with a look of surprise. "We've always been rich? Is that what you said? Rich?"

"You know what I mean."

Bill took a long drink of the beer, lit a cigarette, and said in a dreamy voice, "Naw, we ain't never been rich. We ain't even been close to rich. We ain't never smelled rich, looked rich, acted rich, talked rich, or been rich." He turned and spoke through clenched teeth. "Son, I don't think you got the real drift of all this. We talkin' a four-billion-dollar factory setting up shop in our back yard. They have added another zero to the price of everything in this county. You went to college; you know what happens when they add a zero overnight. One-hundred-fifty dollar land is fifteen-hundred; fifteen-hundred-dollar land is fifteen-thousand; you know what we're talking here? We're rich."

Phillip Zephries winced. "I know, I know."

Bill reached into the pocket of his shirt; he produced a wad of bills. "You know what these are?" He handed the money to his brother. Phillip flipped though the bills. "My God, these are hundred dollar bills. Where'd you get this kind of money?"

"At the bank."

"How?"

"My signature. I own almost three million dollars worth of property. Get it?"

"You . . . You borrowed money on the farm already?"

"As a matter of fact, I own this pickup, a super crop of tobacco, two tractors, and a horse trailer. If you want to call that collateral you can. But, to tell you the truth, since old Saturn started moving in here, my signature is worth more than my collateral. Get it?"

"This is a thousand dollars."

"And it's all yours."

"Mine?"

"Look, Phillip, I want you to get the feel of this thing. You can't seem to get excited over three million dollars, and I'm here to tell you I'm excited about it."

Phillip stuffed the money back into his brother's shirt pocket; he turned from the window of the truck and walked toward one of the dilapidated outhouses. "I want to take a piss."

Bill threw his empty beer can into the back of the pickup and opened another. He lit another cigarette and blew the smoke into the late afternoon breeze.

Phillip returned from the outhouse while still zipping his fly. He looked out across Memorial Highway 31 and spoke softly. "Bill, with all this coming down—this money, this moving, this changing, this uproar, and this gold rush—I want to get a few things out of the way."

"Shoot."

"I think we should make an effort to find our mother."

Bill took a deep pull off his cigarette. He spat into the grass, frowned, and said, "I knew that was coming. Look, buddy, I've told you too many times. We don't have a mother. She ran out on us when we were kids. Can't you get that out of your system? Amanda thinks she's dead anyway."

Phillip stood with his hands in his outside coat pockets. "And maybe she's on skid row in Detroit."

"Okay! Okay! Tell you what. You take your part of the money and look up your mama. Simple as that. If she's alive and needs anything, I'll help out too."

"Don't you ever wonder?"

"When I was a kid, when people would ask about my mama, I cared. I got mad. But everybody knows the story now. They're tired of it and I'm tired of it."

Phillip got into the front seat of the truck. He took a deep breath. "Now, how would we split this money?"

"Fifty-fifty, you and me. Amanda don't want anything on account of her age and taxes and whatever else Sherman Cooper told her to do. Anyway, between you and me, I think Amanda's got plenty of money. Granddaddy Gyp was a big-time mule salesmen in his day, from the way I've heard it. I've never seen the paperwork, but Amanda's done all right."

The conversation was interrupted by squealing tires. An old white Plymouth station wagon came rattling into the park. Bill said, "Oh, hell! It's Gorman Weeds, and he's got Muff and Puff with him."

The station wagon pulled up beside the pickup. Bill Zephries reached under the seat and picked up a long black pistol. He held it just below the window out of sight of the passengers in the car. "Howdy, boys. You all come out here to the park to smell the flowers?"

Gorman Weeds, a tall, blonde-haired man in his late twenties, took a puff of his cigarette. He spoke in a mean voice. "Hey, Phillip, now that you're home, you ought to know something. I've warned your brother about breaking up people's homes. I'm not warning him any more."

Muff and Puff, both unshaven with greasy hair hanging over their protruding foreheads, nodded in agreement.

Bill Zephries laid the barrel of the gun on the truck's window in full view. He spoke in a jovial manner. "Gorman, you can speak to me personally. No need to upset my brother. We came out here to do a little target practicing. Would you stick that cigarette back in your mouth and let me see if I can miss your rotten teeth while I'm shooting it in two?"

The old Plymouth lurched forward with Gorman Weeds cursing behind the wheel. Bill laughed as the car spun onto the highway and headed back to Spring Hill. He looked at Phillip sitting stone still beside him. "What's the matter, Phillip? Don't you like socializing with your old football buddies? You didn't even say hello to your fellow Raiders."

Phillip tossed his beer can into the back of the pickup, "Let's go home and get something to eat."

Bill shifted the pickup into gear, and they drove slowly back toward Sugar Ridge Road. Phillip suddenly said, "Hey, pull over." Bill stopped the truck as Phillip pointed across the road. "What the hell is that? Have they brought a real live carnival in here?"

Bill leaned his head down and looked past Phillip at the multicolored, many-lettered station wagon and trailer of Reverend Joseph Armes. Bill laughed and said, "Naw, that's Preacher Armes's rig. He's back in town now that his prophecy has come true."

"Prophecy?"

"Yeah, remember he used to preach on the sidewalk about space people coming to Spring Hill and causing all kinds of trouble because of the evil ways of the people and so on? Well, he says Saturn is it."

Phillip said, "My God, look at that thing."

The old station wagon and the sixteen-foot trailer hooked behind it were both painted and plastered all over with bumper stickers and crude lettering that spelled out the Bible's admonitions about sinning.

Woe unto ye sinners
Repent
Do not take the Lord's name in vain
Pray now
No smoking
See Rock City
Visit Hanging Rock
Jesus is Lord
The end is near
Dallas Cowboys

And although Reverend Armes had not noticed it, someone had added a small blue sticker with white lettering that read "Shit Happens." It was as if the occupant of the station wagon and trailer had gone mad in decorating the exterior of his traveling domain.

Reverend Joseph Armes had sold the old Maury County homeplace several years before there was any hint of a land boom. He had taken the money from the sale of the farm and bought the small trailer and station wagon to take him on the road to preach the gospel. That was the year he had discovered whiskey as one of God's gifts to preachers.

There were two loudspeaker horns tied to the top of the station wagon and a hand-held microphone that lay on the front seat attached to a long cord. Joseph Armes traveled through Georgia, Florida, and Mississippi preaching from the roadside, at shopping centers, and any other place that he was not hushed by local authorities for disturbing the peace.

Although he was well into the final stages of alcoholism, he still managed a rather comfortable living with his prophecy. People would give him money, car and trailer repairs, and food in abundance. He was still the boney, black-suited character that he had been when he preached Scott Zephries's funeral in February of 1958, the year he had begun his prophecy of space aliens coming to Maury County.

The station wagon and trailer sat silent and forlorn in the fading light of day in Spring Hill.

Bill said quietly, "Our Daddy used to sit and talk to that old dude for hours. He was crazy back then too. I talked to him the other day and he couldn't quite make out who I was. He hits the sauce from daylight to dark. Said he came back to see his prophecy fulfilled."

Phillip turned and stared down the street. "God, can you imagine the life a man like that must lead?"

Joseph Armes opened his eyes inside the little trailer and tried to focus them on an object above his head. A small, plastic-covered light fixture came into his vision. It was the way the preacher knew for sure where he was.

Several times in the past few weeks, since coming back to Spring Hill, he had awakened to imagine that he was in hell. And that the trailer had been sent there with him. He raised up on one elbow and pulled back a dusty curtain. He saw the street by which he had parked and knew that he was still in

Spring Hill. He caught sight of Phillip Zephries staring at the trailer. Although he didn't recognize the young man, he had a flash of cognizance of some kind. His mind went back to a body in a coffin, a tie pulled up tight around the neck, a tall woman beside him, and soot on the ceiling of a room. Being a prophet, he could not determine if this was something that had happened before or something that would happen in the future. He looked closely at the young Phillip Zephries before his mind wandered to his present circumstance. His stomach ached terribly. He had not eaten in three days. He remembered hot biscuits from his mother's oven. He reached for the bottle of whiskey by his bedside and sat up crying for his mother. Or the biscuits. He was not sure which.

He mused on the burdens of prophecy, on Job and Daniel from the Bible, and much suffering.

He had been sleeping in a follower's house in Orlando, Florida, when the vision had come. He had fallen asleep with the TV on. Next morning he had announced to his hosts that he had had a dream that told him he must return to Spring Hill. His prophecy was about to be fulfilled, and he had to save the city from the space people who were about to invade it. He was totally amazed at his own accuracy when he arrived in town one spring day to find that the invaders were from Saturn.

At dinner that evening at the Old Zephries Place, the matter of selling real estate was dropped. There was talk of the old days when Phillip, because of his shy nature, had become his younger brother's follower. It was Bill who threw Phillip in the Duck River and taught him to swim.

It was Bill who cheered the loudest when Phillip became the quarterback for the Spring Hill Raiders football team. It was Bill who learned to curse, smoke, drink, and chase the girls. Phillip, the achiever of the family, accepted Bill's leadership and bravado with good humor and some awe.

They sat on the front porch after dinner and ate Til's homemade ice cream. It was Til who seemed to realize the import of the gathering. She licked her ice cream spoon and said, "I can feel de chill. Can y'all feel de chill?"

Bill said, "Til, it's seventy degrees out here."

"Maybe so. Maybe so. But I can feel de chill."

At the Poplar House restaurant in downtown Spring Hill, a fashionable young couple sat in one of the booths contemplating the dinner menu. It was the shoes, the jewelry, the casual manner in which their expensive cotton coats hung from the backs of nearby chairs that made observers think these people were well-to-do and not from Spring Hill. The man and woman were just over thirty. The woman was bored. "Please listen carefully, Jeffrey. I don't want to shout." She leaned toward the man. "There is nothing on this menu that I would dare eat."

He whispered in turn, "What's wrong?"

"This stuff is loaded with cholesterol and triglycerides. Everything is fried."

The man did not look up from his menu. He spoke flatly. "Have a salad and a glass of water."

The woman threw the menu down on the table. "What in

the world are we doing here in this godforsaken wide place in the road? We could have at least gone to Nashville. There's nothing in this town, and we've been here all day just looking at one rock and tree after another. I don't see what you see here. It's nothing, absolutely nothing."

"It's history in the making."

"It's boredom in the apocalypse. So they're going to build a factory here, the Civil War was fought here, someday they are going to turn on the lights after dark, someday the population will explode to twelve hundred people." The woman leaned toward her husband in mock excitement. "Let's come back then. Let's leave now and come back then."

The waitress at the Poplar House restaurant was suddenly standing beside the booth with pen and pad poised. "Your order, please?"

The man looked up and said, "Cheeseburger, fries, and a Coke."

The waitress made a note on the pad, turned to the woman, and gave her a questioning look. The woman said, "The same, please. And I'll have coffee afterward."

The waitress asked, "Will that be all?"

The man spoke, "Yes, that's all, thank you." He looked at his wife. "No triwhatchacallits in hamburgers?"

The woman pretended not to hear the remark. She looked appraisingly around the room, "You know, these people do have a certain charm. Do you suppose they mind being photographed?"

The man followed her gaze around the room with his own. He said, "Bullshit."

Next morning after breakfast, Amanda called the family into the front parlor of the old house. She said, "Til, you come in too. This concerns all of us."

She sat at a small rolltop desk and chewed on a yellow pencil. She waited until all were seated before speaking. "Have you boys talked now? Do you want to sell this place?"

The abruptness of her statement took the young men by surprise. Bill said, "I think my deal is out in the open. It's not trying to figure out *if* we're gonna sell, it's when."

Phillip got up, walked to the front door and opened it on a drizzly, cool November morning. He turned back to the trio seated in the parlor. "If this place is worth what we think it is, and I believe what I've heard, I'm not going to need my job." He hurried on, "I know it sounds stupid, but I spent four years in college making plans. Now all of that's out the window. It's frustrating to suddenly have to change my thinking. Oh, hell, I don't know what I'm trying to say."

Bill coughed and crossed his legs. Eyes turned to him. He said, "I'm not stupid. I know the difference selling this place is gonna make. I've got tobacco coming in case right now. It's gotta be stripped, I know that, and I'm gonna do it too. We don't have to change anything just because we come into a little money." He threw up his hands and smiled at Phillip. "Why don't you buy the damned place where you work?"

Phillip scratched his head. He spoke in a firm clear voice. "Okay, I guess we have to do it. Let's sell."

Amanda Zephries shook her hands as if to shoo away a fly. "Okay, okay, let's do first things first. Looks like Til and I will have to find a place to live. We'll worry about that later. I want Sherman Cooper to handle all the legal work. Sherman is an old and trusted friend of the family and has taken care of us all these years, and I believe he can take care of the paperwork for us. Do any of you have any better idea?"

The trio looked at one another. Til said, "If we leavin', we gonna dig up them azalea bushes and take 'em with us. I sweated over 'em too long to leave 'em here to be mowed down."

Amanda said, "There'll be a lot of little things to care of, but let's do them one at a time."

Til went to bring some coffee into the room. The four sat talking for almost an hour, sharing memories of the old days. They talked together in the parlor of the old house as if awaiting a storm.

Bill drove off in his pickup to round up some help in stripping his tobacco, the final phase of preparing the crops for market. Amanda asked Til to take her to do some shopping in Spring Hill. Phillip said he would like to hang around the house and do some reading.

Left alone, Phillip took a long walk around the property. He felt as though he were visiting an old friend for the last time. The soft rain added to the melancholy of the day.

Phillip had not walked far when he came to the old fence where his father had died, tangled in the wire. The posts had rotted and the wire had rusted, but the old fence still resisted total decay. As young boys the two sons of Scott Zephries had avoided the area. Phillip thought of how odd it was that life was so resilient, man so tough and durable, and yet a life could be snuffed out in seconds. He tried to imagine the scene as it was on the day of the accident. It was so long ago, another time, another era. Yet he could see it as clearly as the winter skyline of hills and trees laid bare by falling leaves. He had always been surprised to see the rocks, the hillsides, and the streams that came into view when the leaves fell. And now he stood feeling unprotected from the outside world. An old barn on a far away hillside was visible in the gray afternoon. Phillip thought of how his grandmother, Amanda, had said that he and

Bill were as different as summer and winter. Bill was the summer boy. While Phillip always had a dread of the unknown lurking just below the surface of his personality, Bill seemed secure and carefree. He seldom looked at newspapers or magazines except for news of the tobacco market or pictures of pretty girls. He cared little about local or national politics or events. The closest he had come to a political statement was when he had said he would never vote for a man who didn't smoke.

Phillip remembered the time during the Cuban missile crisis when he asked Bill if he had heard the news. Bill had snorted and said that the news was for niggers and Jews.

Phillip stepped over the fence where his father had been shot and wondered what had happened to the gun. It was natural for things of that kind to fall to Bill. No one had ever mentioned suicide to either of the sons, but the nature and the timing of his father's death had always made Phillip wonder. It was one of those family skeletons that had remained in the conversational closet all through the years.

It was good land that the young man hiked across on that drizzly afternoon. Large tracts of timber, wide spaces of pasture land, and long road frontage. It was what a real estate agent could fairly call "gently rolling."

Phillip walked for almost an hour, stopping now and then to recall some childhood pleasure he had taken on the land. He finally made a left turn and then another until he was headed back toward the old house. His shoes were beginning to soak up the chilled wetness of the grass and leaves.

He returned to the house, changed into dry clothes, and fell asleep while reading. It was some time later that he awakened to the phone ringing. He made his way to the kitchen and lifted the receiver from its hook on the wall. "Hello."

"Pardon me, is this the Zephries residence?"

"Yes."

"Is there a Mister Phillip Zephries there?"

"This is he."

"Ah, well, you're the one I wanted to speak with. Mister Zephries, this is George Atworth."

"What can I do for you?"

"I'd like to see you and talk to you."

"Are you in the real estate business?"

"Uh, no. No, I'm not in the real estate business. Uh, Mister Zephries, this is an important phone call. I can't tell you what it's about right now. Could you meet me at the Holiday Inn in Columbia this afternoon at four?"

"Why would I want to do that?"

"Mister Zephries, this call is about your mother. Meet me at the Holiday Inn at four this afternoon. Come alone. Go to the front desk and ask for Mr. Atworth. Good-bye."

Phillip heard the phone click as he started to ask another question. He hung up and stared at the phone. It was three-fifteen and Columbia was fifteen minutes away. All kinds of thoughts started running through his mind. Maybe his mother was in town. Maybe she had heard of the property selling. Maybe she had heard Phillip was in town. There were many other thoughts, none of them positive. He ran up the stairs to his room. He needed a shave and a shower.

At three-forty Phillip was dressed and driving down Sugar Ridge Road. As he came to the junction of Depot Street and Main Street, he saw Til's car parked by the side of the road. Til sat in the front seat. He yelled at her, "Where's Amanda?"

Til leaned out the car window. "She went in de library. Said she be right out. You want to see her?"

"No. No, I don't need her. Say, do we know anybody named George Atworth?"

Til scratched her head. "No, I never heard of nobody by dat name."

"Okay, I'll be back for supper. Bye!"

"Uh huh."

Phillip swung the rental car right on the way to the Columbia Holiday Inn. Just then, Amanda came out of the library and got into Til's car. "Was that Phillip?"

"Uh huh."

"Where's he going in such a hurry?"

"He didn't say. Wanted to know if we knowed a man name of Atworth."

"Atworth? Did you say Atworth?"

"Uh huh."

"My God! Oh, my God!"

CHAPTER FOUR

BROTHERHOOD

Phillip parked his rental car in front of the Holiday Inn in Columbia. The rain was heavier now. He sat looking at the construction work that seemed to be going on everywhere in the area. He could still feel the rivalry that had existed between this larger town and his own of Spring Hill. He remembered a football cheer that used to irk him:

Spring Hill you're it!
Spring Hill you're it!
S. H. for Spring Hill
I. T. for it!

He jumped from the car, slammed the door, and ran through the rain to the cover of the motel lobby. He took the lapels of his jacket in both hands and shook off the rain. He looked around the lobby for a person he might recognize. There were two older people at the check-in desk. A young lady sat in one of the chairs and read a newspaper. No one seemed to notice him.

When the older couple had checked in and left, Phillip walked up to the desk and said, "Hi, I'm Phillip Zephries. I'm supposed to meet a Mister Atworth here at four."

The young lady behind the counter turned and picked up a note from a table. She handed it to him and said, "Yes sir,

Mister Atworth left a message for you."

Phillip thanked her and glanced down at the message which read, "I'll be in the Apples lounge." It was signed George Atworth.

There were only a few people in the lounge when Phillip walked into the dim atmosphere. A large-screen television was to his left. Two men sat talking at the bar. The lady bartender was slicing lemons, putting out small dishes of snacks, and preparing for the day's work. A young black man sat in the far right-hand corner of the lounge. He arose from his table and said, "Mister Zephries? Over here."

Phillip made his way to the man's table and stood staring at his outstretched hand for a moment. "Atworth? Are you George Atworth?"

The black man motioned for him to sit down, "Yes sir, that's me. Have a seat."

Phillip suddenly felt angry and his voice reflected it. "What is this all about?"

The black man was calm and composed. "Relax, Mister Zephries. I'll explain everything. Believe me."

Phillip seemed reluctant to take his seat, but he did. He folded his hands on the table, glared at the black man, and said, "Talk."

George Atworth said, "I think I'll have a beer. Want one?"

Phillip spoke angrily, "Talk."

The black man called to the waitress, "Miller beer, please." He looked at Phillip, "You?"

Phillip said, "Two."

They sat silent while the waitress brought the beer. George Atworth gave her some money and said, "Keep the change."

The black stranger sipped his beer and said, "Mister Zephries, I'm a reporter for the Commocorp News Syndicate. I'm here to do a story on the Saturn plant. Well, not the plant itself, but the social impact the plant will have on the area."

Phillip pushed the beer aside and leaned forward with a grim expression. "I want to know what you know about my family, how you think you know, and why you know?"

For the first time the black man sounded angry. He held up his hands and said, "Hey, man, cool it. You know, I'm getting to that. Give me a minute. Okay?"

Phillip's hand shook as he picked up his beer and leaned back in his chair. "Okay, talk."

George Atworth took a cigarette from a gold case, lit it, and blew a puff of white smoke toward the ceiling of the lounge. He spoke as if he meant to take his time. He said, "Phillip . . ." Phillip winced at the familiarity.

"Phillip, I think there's a big story here. The Zephries family being just a small part. Do you realize that twenty-five thousand new people are going to be moving into this area? With those numbers in mind, Spring Hill's eleven hundred people will be in the minority. There will be Jews, Blacks, Italians, Germans, Poles, and all manner of different cultures coming here. I'm interested in the sociological impact all of these people are going to make. Mind you, I have my own prejudice. I think these are good people, family people; people who want schools, hospitals, recreation, and social intercourse for their children. These people are not going to come here and hide behind the walls of Saturn. They'll want to live and retire here. We might mention that some of your own people will be coming back here. And to be honest, from the research I've done, many of them don't want to come back to these hills; especially the children who are used to living in a modern urban area. There's one report — "

Phillip slapped his hand on the table. "Mister, will you get to the point? I want to hear what you know about my mother!"

George Atworth calmly put out his cigarette in the ashtray. His voice became quiet and firm. "Phillip . . ." The man paused. "How should I put this? Uh, I know your mother well.

When she left Spring Hill those many years ago, she came to Detroit and took a job as a receptionist in a hospital. There she met a doctor. After a two-year courtship, they were married and a year later had a son. Three years later that doctor died. Your grandmother, Amanda, knows this story. I understand that she has never shared it with you." George Atworth took a deep breath, as if he had rehearsed the speech. He continued, "I'm trying to communicate to you that I know what I'm doing. I asked for this assignment. I am not a nigger field hand or a car washer. I know what Spring Hill is all about, and I know what you're all about." He rubbed the back of his neck and twisted his head from side to side. He lowered his voice as he leaned across the table. "Phillip, that doctor your mother married was black. He was my father. I am your brother."

Phillip Zephries felt a sharp pain in his left temple. He put his hand to the side of his head and steadied himself. He was dizzy and wide-eyed. He held his hand in front of his face for a second. He realized that he believed the man. There was something in the voice and in the face that told Phillip Zephries that this man was indeed his brother. He tried to summon a sense of disbelief. His mind was forming sentences that his mouth could not utter. He was surprised by his own voice when he whispered, "Well, I'll be damned. I'll be damned."

George Atworth sat looking calmly at his half-brother. He had not wanted to seem angry or bitter. He leaned back in his seat and grimaced. A sense of relief came over him now that it was in the open and done with. He shrugged his shoulders. "Do you want to hear the rest of the story?"

Phillip Zephries studied the face of his half-brother. He heard himself saying, "Yes, please, tell me the whole story."

Phillip sat mesmerized as George Atworth chronicled his mother's past. She had gone to Detroit and had taken a job as a receptionist in young doctor George R. Atworth's office.

They had married two years later. There was one son from the union, George Roger Atworth, Jr., born in May of '61.

In 1964, Doctor George Atworth died in an automobile accident. He left his entire estate to his wife and son. The woman, widowed for the second time and without support, entered the real estate profession. She used her inheritance to build a considerable fortune.

George Atworth told the story in a flat, unemotional voice, counting off the incidents in his mother's life on his fingers. When he came to the last little finger of his left hand, he slapped his hands together in finality and said, "That's the story."

Phillip Zephries suddenly blinked and shook his head as if he had been dreaming. "Where is she now?"

George Atworth said, "I have a message for you, and for Bill. She said she would get in touch with you when she could feel right about it. Said she had some things to do."

"Do you mean to tell me that you know where she is and you won't tell?"

"That's right. I'm sorry, but she made me promise. But she's fine. In good health and has plenty enough money."

"How does she . . . er, I mean — "

"She sends her love to the both of you."

Phillip stared at the beer bottle in his hand and made small circles of moisture on the tabletop with it. He glanced up at his half-brother and said, "Small world, ain't it?"

Amanda stood on the front porch of the Old Zephries Place and watched as a late model Cadillac entered the drive. She waved as a tall, white-haired man emerged from the driver's seat. Sherman Andrew Cooper, lawyer, financial adviser, and longtime friend of Amanda Zephries, spoke in a sophisticated southern voice. "'Lo, Amanda. I came as soon as I got your message."

The two embraced for a moment before entering the house where Amanda led the way to the parlor. Sherman Cooper laid his raincoat across the back of a chair. He spoke quietly. "Are we alone?"

"Yes. Til's gone out and Bill is stripping tobacco. It's Phillip I'm worried about."

"So you think Rosanna's other son has shown up here?"

"It has to be him. Who else could it be with that name?" Amanda Zephries wrung her hands as she paced the floor. "Lord, Sherman, I've dreaded this day for as long as I've kept this terrible secret. I've rehearsed my speech a thousand sleepless nights. I knew the boys would find out someday. And now I'm frightened. What am I to do?"

Sherman Cooper brushed a pipe ash from his expensive suit jacket. "Let's cross these bridges as we get to them. When Phillip returns, we'll let him talk first. We'll go from there. You have done these boys no harm. You have done their half-brother no harm. You have merely kept the secret a little too long. No crime in that; none at all. Why don't you use up some of that nervous energy fixing a cup of coffee for me?"

Amanda left the room to make the coffee. Sherman crossed one long leg over the other and sat back in his chair. He was an angular man. He wore a slim, tailored, gray suit from New York City, maroon silk tie over a fine cotton shirt, and comfortable yet fashionable shoes.

His life had been unspectacular as far as the public was concerned. But Sherman Cooper was an unusual man. One tragic moment in his life had transformed it forever. At the start of his honeymoon trip, his young bride at his side, Sherman drove a new Ford Roadster past an intersection at the precise moment that a huge truck failed to stop for a traffic sign. The truck came from his right. He instinctively jerked the wheel to the left to avoid the collision. The truck swerved to the right just far enough to clip the right side of the car and take off the door. His wife was thrown from the car into the roadside ditch. She would be paralyzed from the waist down for life. Sherman sustained some small cuts and bruises.

After a lengthy recuperation, Alvena Bostic Cooper, daughter of the wealthy Alva Bostic who made his fortune in real estate and the operation of a limestone quarry, returned home from the hospital to take up her married life with Sherman Cooper, attorney at law.

They were a familiar couple around Nashville social circles. He, tall and handsome, walking along behind her wheelchair. She, small and serene, wrapped in a variety of exotic lap covers. They remained married until her death of pneumonia in 1962. Sherman Cooper never remarried.

The young lawyer's work took him around the state of Tennessee where he discreetly made the acquaintance of a number of young widows and divorcees. He was never unfaithful to his wife within the boundaries of Davidson County.

The quiet of the Old Zephries Place was interrupted by the harsh sound of automobile tires on the gravel of the driveway. Amanda rushed to the window of the parlor. "It's him . . . it's Phillip. My God, he knows, he knows!"

The two conspirators stood silent and grim as they heard the front door open and footsteps coming toward the parlor.

Phillip entered the room and stopped abruptly when he saw the tense faces of his grandmother and Sherman Cooper. He put his hands in the outside pockets of his coat and stared at his feet. He spoke quietly and angrily. "You two knew all along, didn't you? I've just met my brother George." He slammed his fist into the side of the door, drawing blood from his knuckles. "Dammit, do you realize what it's like to learn something like that this late in life?"

Phillip's outburst was interrupted by the slamming of the kitchen door. Bill Zephries hollered through the house, "Anybody home?"

Phillip turned disgustedly toward the voice. "We're in here. In the parlor."

Bill Zephries entered the room from the hallway near the kitchen. "Hey! What you all doin' in here? Hi, Sherman."

"Hi, Bill. How's the tobacco coming?"

"Well, I got a few frog-eyes from all this rain, but it's in good case and the stripping is going good. I'm baling this year."

Bill looked around the room. He looked from Phillip's long face to the sad expression of Amanda. "Hey, you all okay? You guys look like your dog died. Where's Til?"

Amanda spoke, "Til's fine. We're all fine. We have to talk." She looked at the floor.

Sherman Cooper knocked the ashes from his pipe into the palm of his hand. He threw them into the fireplace and said, "Why don't we all have a seat?"

Bill sat down on the arm of a high-backed leather chair. "Is there somethin' wrong with the deed to the farm? Is that all okay?"

Sherman Cooper said, "That's all in good order. Just sit still a minute."

The lawyer took his stance in the middle of the room. He cleared his throat and spoke solemnly. "Now, I've known you boys since you were pups. I've known Amanda since before your granddaddy passed away. I've seen this family come through with some tough action when things got rough. Now, this is going to require some love and understanding."

Bill looked at Phillip. "What's this all about?"

Phillip said, "We've got a black brother. Mama went off and married a black man and we've got a black brother named George. I just had a beer with him. He is our brother and he is black."

Sherman Cooper spoke into the stunned silence. "Half-brother. He's a half-brother."

Bill Zephries jumped to his feet. "What the hell are you talking about?" He snapped at his grandmother, "Amanda, what is he talking about?"

Amanda Zephries stood tall and spoke haltingly. "It's true. What Phillip said is true. I've known it for many years. I just could never find the right time to . . ."

Bill Zephries threw his hands to the ceiling. "That bitch! That no good whore! That damned slut! For crying out loud!" He turned to Phillip who sat with his head in his hands. "Well, little brother, you wanna go suck on your mama's tit now?"

Sherman Cooper put his hand on Bill's shoulder. "Bill, please, your grandmother, please."

Bill Zephries wiped the sweat from his brow. "Where is the son of a bitch? I'll kill the nigger bastard!"

Phillip Zephries kicked hard at the paneled parlor door. The loud clatter quieted the room. He said in a calm voice, "Listen, listen carefully. I'm only going to tell this story once."

With only an occasional muttering of an epithet from Bill, Phillip finished the story as George Atworth had told it to him. In the long conversation that followed, the four people in the room found themselves to be in a quandary about the motives of George Atworth and the whereabouts of Rosanna Zephries-Atworth.

George Atworth walked to the small counter at the Spring Hill Library and spoke to the lady in charge. "Pardon me, but do you have a city map of Spring Hill?"

Without looking up from her chore, the lady replied, "We haven't had any maps for a while. We gave them all away during the gold rush. You might try City Hall. It's up there behind the Cedar Inn Restaurant."

The people at City Hall were moving from their small offices to a trailer provided the city by Governor Alexander. They could not find a map.

George Atworth walked back down to the main thoroughfare. He stopped a man about to enter his pickup truck. "Pardon me, sir. I want to drive around Spring Hill and get a good look at it. Could you tell me which way I should go?"

The man looked at the nattily attired black man and asked, "Where you parked?"

George Atworth pointed to his car at the curb. The man said, "Get up on top of your car and look around. You can see the whole damned town. Save you some gas." The man slammed the door of the pickup and drove away.

The young black man spent the next thirty minutes walking north toward the Williamson County line and back south to his car. He wore a lightweight waterproof jacket and a pair of comfortable walking shoes. The rain had stopped but the early evening was chilly and damp. He counted six churches, three real estate offices, and two traffic lights. He passed the station wagon and trailer of Preacher Joseph Armes. He stood reading the bumper stickers and Bible quotations splattered all over the two. He was so taken by the sight that he kept staring at it as he walked and subsequently bumped into a parked car. He bent over, rubbing his knee and muttering a profanity. He finally smiled at himself, looked back toward the trailer, and said, "Sorry about that."

When George Atworth returned to his rental car, he sat in

the driver's seat and pulled some papers from his briefcase. He had written a piece that he wanted to send back to his home office. George Atworth understood that the Detroit press was favorably inclined toward any enterprise that had to do with the manufacture of automobiles. It was not the story he would have liked to file. The boss had wanted a human interest story and had promised him a byline in Sunday's magazine section if it turned out to be, as the boss had put it, "witty and charming."

He wanted to read it again in the ambience of the small town of which he was writing. He switched on the map light and started reading to himself:

General Motors Comes to the South

George Atworth
Spring Hill, Tenn.

On July 31, 1985, General Motors announced that Saturn was coming to Spring Hill, Tennessee. Not the planet, the plant. The planet is 886 million miles away. If it started this way at the speed of light, this generation could ignore the start of the journey. But the plant is another matter. It is headed this way from Detroit, Michigan, at the speed of a small automobile. It will be here soon. The plant will be 150 acres of high technology under one roof. Plans are drawn and offices have been built to house the people who are going to build the plant. The office units cost one million dollars. This leaves General Motors with a planned budget of three billion and some odd million, as they say here in Spring Hill.

The people who did not know that Saturn was a planet thought perhaps it was Saturn the Roman God of agriculture. They figured the god would have more business here on this fertile land than General Motors. God is very big in Spring Hill, but Lord, this is Chevy country; NASCAR Champion Daryl Waltrip lives just down the road in Franklin, and he drives one.

The plant will use five million gallons of water a day; that is an astounding amount of water for anything other than a brewery. The water will come from the Duck River and probably wind up in Carter's Creek after it has passed through General Motors. One local said this reminded him of what happens to oats once they have been through a horse.

The first Saturn automobile is to roll off the line in 1989. It will cost two thousand dollars less than a comparable automobile made the old-fashioned way. The plant will employ six thousand people; this, plus satellite industries, will swell the population in the Spring Hill area to about twenty-five thousand. In early 1985, the population of Spring Hill was eleven hundred.

Now the land boom is nearly over in Maury County. Every piece of property between Columbia and Nashville has been regarded as an investment (Spring Hill is located between Nashville and Columbia on State Route 31). A lot of land has changed hands in the past year. It was a windfall for local real estate agents and owners. There are still a few for-sale signs on lawns, but the boom is bust.

And guess who's coming to dinner ... the United Auto Workers. General Motors signed an agreement with them before they made the final announcement that Saturn had landed in Spring Hill. There was some question as to the legality of the agreement, but it was done. GM says there will be a lot of jobs for the local people. Skeptics say that GM built a Corvette plant in Bowling Green, Kentucky, and that they brought UAW members in to run the plant and did not use many locals. Tennessee is a right-to-work state.

Not much has been done to measure or deal with the sociological impact that Saturn will have on the once sleepy little town of Spring Hill. On the contrary, much effort went into ignoring Spring Hill as a city until Mayor George Jones and the city fathers talked of annexing the Saturn site and taxing GM accordingly. Tennessee governor Lamar Alexander and General Motors talked them out of such a bold move. GM will pay in-lieu-of-taxes. That is to say that they will pay a fixed amount of money to Maury County; Spring Hill will get some of that money.

After the deal had been struck, consumer advocate Ralph Nader came to Columbia, the seat of Maury County, and made what some locals refer to as one of his "shuda speeches"; he told Maury Countians what they should have done.

Why was Spring Hill selected as the site for Saturn? General Motors spokesman Stanley Hall said the area was chosen because it was near consumers. GM plans to build cars on order and get them out to the customer in record time. One Spring Hill resident said that GM was trying to imitate McDonald's. If the adjective didn't jar the sentence so much, you could say that this is the beginning of the first fast-car franchise.

The state of Tennessee will build a multi-million-dollar parkway from I-65 to the Saturn plant. It will be possible to work at the plant until retirement and never experience the aesthetic charm of Spring Hill.

There are signs posted everywhere around the Spring Hill area welcoming Saturn. A song has been written about the event, T-shirts display the Saturn emblem, and the prospects for booming business are excellent.

If GM seems aloof from all the speculation surrounding its coming, perhaps it has a right. The building of a $3.5 billion plant is concern enough.

The story here is this: For so many years, since the advent of the industrial revolution in America, southerners have packed up and moved north to find jobs in the factories. Now they, the factories and the jobs, are coming to the South. Once entire families migrated north. The communities formed by groups of white and black southerners were once known as Little Georgia, Little Kentucky, Little West Virginia. Those groups that once huddled together ghetto-like on the cultural fringes of the big industrial cities of America will now sleep in the beds of their ancestors, live in their childhood homes, and walk to work if they please. No more humiliation by sophisticated Yankees. No more long, lonesome letters home. No more bragging on the red, white-walled, eight-cylindered Chevy parked in the back yard. General Motors will be parked in the back yard.

Will there be Little Detroits? Little New Yorks? Little Indianas? The prospect looms rich in human experience and adventure.

Will there be demeaning southern tricks played on the Yankee immigrants? Will they go to a restaurant, order sweetbreads, and expect a selection of cakes and cookies? Will they order the popular local dish of rooster fries and expect some kind of omelet? Will they be forced into cultural isolation in their own southern ghettos? Most likely not. They will mix and mingle into the culture of the South. They will be welcome everywhere. The ladies will attend cocktail parties where they will learn to talk with their hand-held fans and enjoy mint juleps. They will learn to glisten (southern women never sweat).

The northern gentlemen will learn the difference between a mare, a foal, a stud, a cow, a heifer, a bull, a mule, and a Republican.

The Yankees will learn to sleep with an open window. They will find that they are respected and appreciated for their honest labor. They will learn the difference between servility and civility (the reputed secret of the South).

And one fine morning, late in the spring, while sleeping by that open window, the sweet smell of magnolias will fill the air and seep into their consciousness, and they will know why so many folks like it down here.

All agree that GM and all who work for GM are welcome here. They are welcome to the fresh air, the sunshine, and the singing of bluebirds. It is with some smug satisfaction that the southerners realize that the best working environment is here. Nissan has a large plant in Smyrna, Tennessee, and Toyota is building a plant in Kentucky. How beautiful, in that southern way of thinking, that Spring Hill, and the South, will finally be able to say, "On a clear day, you really can see General Motors."

—30—

Sally Weeds was in her trailer less than a mile away. She was angry at Bill Zephries because he was late again. She was dressed and ready for dinner at Cajun's Wharf in Nashville. Bill had promised to pick her up at five-thirty, and it was already a little past six. Sally did not own a car. She either walked to where she wanted to go in Spring Hill or waited for Bill Zephries. She peered through the window for a sign of her lover as she adjusted her clothing and fluffed her hair. She would not wait much longer.

Phillip Zephries had ridden to Columbia with his brother Bill and had managed to calm him down. Bill was no longer talking of killing George Atworth. There was still anger and frustration between the two. Bill said he wanted to know "right now" what the man was up to.

Phillip explained that George Atworth was really a reporter, that he had asked for the assignment, and that he didn't believe the man wanted any money or part of the real estate holdings.

Bill Zephries was more skeptical. He believed the man was in Spring Hill for something other than a story. "That s.o.b. is up to no damned good. You can bet your ass on that."

Sally Weeds slammed the door of her trailer and locked it. She walked quickly down Beechcroft, turned right at the Episcopal Church, and headed south. She wore a hooded raincoat, jeans, a sweater, and a pair of knee-high boots. She turned as she saw a car approaching and stuck up her thumb. Her intention was to hitch a ride to Columbia and teach Bill Zephries a lesson. Several cars passed her.

George Atworth had spent the last few minutes driving some of the back roads in Spring Hill. He caught the figure of Sally Weeds in his headlights and pulled to the side of the road. It was difficult to tell if the hitchhiker was a man or a woman, but George felt the need to talk to some of the locals and figured a hitchhiker would be perfect. He rolled down the window. "I'm going as far as Columbia," he said.

Sally Weeds stepped from the sidewalk, opened the car door, and scooted into the front seat. She reached above her head and removed the hood of the raincoat. "That's where I'm going, thank you."

George Atworth put the car in motion as Sally Weeds turned her head to look at him. She caught her breath. "Why, you . . . you're a . . . you're colored."

George Atworth smiled. "I've noticed that. I'm a reporter from Detroit. I'm staying at the Holiday Inn in Columbia. You want me to stop, or do you want a ride?"

Sally Weeds moved closer to her side of the door, looked out at the cool, damp evening, and said, "No, go on. I need to get over there." She stared at the neat black man in the driver's seat as she shook her head to loosen her hair. "Are you from around here? Did you play football at Spring Hill or Columbia?" George Atworth lit a cigarette and offered her one from the gold case. "No, thank you. That's not my brand." She retrieved one of her own cigarettes and lit it. "I'm not supposed to be riding around with you. You know that, don't you?"

"I am very much aware of that fact. But you are not riding around with me. I am giving you a lift to Columbia."

Sally Weeds shifted in her seat and continued to stare. "You sure you're not from around here someplace?"

"I was born in Detroit, grew up there, went to college there, and this is my first time in Tennessee."

"You a reporter, huh?"

"Yes, I am. And if you don't mind, I'd like to ask you a few questions."

"About what?"

"About the Saturn plant."

"Oh, really! You want to ask me what I think?"

"Yes, I'd be very interested in what you think."

"Well, that's a new twist. There's been a thousand reporters down here, and the only thing any of 'em ever asked me was what time I got off, and that includes one of the women reporters."

"What do you do?"

"I tell 'em to go to hell. I've got a steady boyfriend."

"I see. What I meant was, where do you work?"

"I'm not workin' anywhere right now. I do waitress work mostly, one place or another. My ex is a real mean son of a bitch. Everwhere I get a job, he comes in and starts trouble and I get fired. I wish he'd just drop dead."

"What do you think of Saturn coming here?"

"I say let it come. The more the merrier. The bigger the better."

"Do you plan to work there?"

"Lord, no, I'm not a factory person. You notice I'm not in Detroit, don't you? When the money starts rolling in I'm gonna open me a joint and get some of that easy money. My boy-friend is gonna buy me a Jeep and put me in the beer joint business when he closes his real estate deal pretty soon. I can make money off my looks, if I do say so myself. I worked in Nashville for two months one time. Made a bundle on tips too. Course there's not anybody in Nashville but a bunch of pissant lawyers and businessmen. Not anybody to talk to in Nashville." Sally Weeds went silent for a moment, then laughed. "Come to think of it, they talk like you over there."

"It's only thirty miles from here, isn't it?"

"Well, it might as well be on the moon, as far as I'm concerned. Over here the waitresses don't give the men any-thing to look at. When I open my lounge I'm gonna give 'em something to look at like they do in Nashville. That's where you get your tips. I'm good at it, if I do say so myself."

"Doesn't it worry you that it's going to spoil the neighbor-hood to bring all of those strange people into it?"

Sally Weeds laughed again. "My God, have you ever seen Spring Hill, Tennessee? The way they talk now you'd think Jesus was born here. This town is as dead on Saturday night as any 'possum you see alongside this road. They're gonna come down here and spend so many billion dollars and worry about Spring Hill? They ought to plow it under and make a parking lot out of it. The only time anybody ever comes out of these woods to Spring Hill is when they need a doctor or a haircut.

Hey, you can let me out up here at the bowling alley on the right."

George Atworth sat silent for a moment. He slowed the car and looked across the seat at Sally Weeds. "I'd really like to continue the interview for a few minutes if you don't mind. You have some very honest attitudes about this thing."

Sally's face took on a serious look. "Hey, don't use all this stuff. I'm just talking."

"I don't have to use your name. I just want to get some impressions of what the average person thinks of a big social change like this."

Sally Weeds looked uncomfortable. "Well, you can drive on through Columbia if you want to for a few minutes, but stay in town and drive around. Don't leave the main road."

"I won't. I'll be happy to bring you right back here."

"Ten minutes tops."

George Atworth flipped on the map light and scribbled a few notes in shorthand on a legal pad that lay between them. Sally Weeds looked at the notes suspiciously. "Is that all I said?"

"No, no, that's just a sort of reminder."

Sally spoke as if she had been insulted. "I know what shorthand is. I took a little of it in high school. I thought one time I'd like to work in an office and be a secretary. But that's not for me. I'm a good-time girl. I couldn't stand to sit on my butt all day and talk on the phone. The way I figure it, people got to have a good time or there's no sense of working. It's like my boyfriend says—it's dirty work but somebody's got to do it." Sally laughed. "That's a joke."

George Atworth managed a chuckle. "Tell me about your boyfriend. I mean, do a lot of people here who make money in real estate buy new cars or use the money to start up new enterprises like your, uh, lounge?"

"Well, some of the folks are old, you know. They just take the money and run to the bank with it. Some get new cars and go someplace else and buy another house where it's not so high to live. Most of them buy Datsuns or Toyotas around here. Isn't that funny? Chevy comes in here and builds a big plant and starts throwing money around and the people use it to buy Jap cars. Lord, I'll tell you, this is strange country, if you ask me."

Phillip and Bill Zephries had spent a couple of hours hanging around the Holiday Inn in Columbia. They had had several beers in the Apple lounge while waiting for George Atworth to return so they could question him about his motives. Bill had grown more interested in George Atworth's motives than his color. He was convinced that there was some kind of conspiracy in the half-brother's coming to Spring Hill.

Phillip and Bill finally gave up the vigil at the Holiday Inn and were returning to Spring Hill on Route 31. Phillip had elected to drive as Bill had done most of the drinking. Bill sat slouched in the front seat of Phillip's rental car. He suddenly jerked upright and said, "What? What was . . . ? Hey! Did you scc that? Who was in that car? That was Sally. And she's with some guy! What is this? Pull over here."

Phillip spun his head around and looked back at the tail lights of the car that carried George Atworth and Sally Weeds. Bill was yelling for him to pull over. Phillip kept driving. "You're seeing things. You had too much to drink. You can't see who's in that car."

Bill was on his knees in the front seat glaring back down the road at the disappearing car. "They had a light on in there. I saw 'em bigger 'n Dallas. That's Sally in that car."

Phillip kept driving. "Look, I've had a big day. I'm tired of this. I'll take you back to your truck. Sally's probably waiting for you in the trailer."

69

Bill went on, "By God, I've known Sally Weeds all my life. If that ain't her in that car, it's her twin sister. Hurry up."

Phillip stepped on the accelerator and quickly covered the nine miles between Spring Hill and Columbia. As he approached the left turn on Depot Street, he asked, "You want to go by Sally's trailer or get your truck?"

"Get my truck."

"Okay."

As soon as Phillip had stopped the car in the driveway of the Old Zephries Place, Bill was out the door and into his pickup. Phillip yelled, "Be careful out there. You've had a few. Call me when you find Sally."

Bill hollered over the roar of the pickup engine, "Don't sweat it."

As Bill's pickup rattled down Sugar Ridge Road, Phillip noticed that Sherman Cooper's car was still in the driveway. He sat in the car for a silent minute. "Those two old connivers have been talking a long time," he thought.

The wet weeds alongside the pathway brushed against Phillip's pants leg as he walked to the door of the old house. He knocked gently on the door. Amanda came at once. She cracked it open and was surprised to see her grandson. "My goodness, Phillip, what are you knocking for?

"Well, I just . . ."

"In all the years you've lived here you've never knocked. Come in. Come in, for goodness sakes. Where's Bill?"

Phillip stepped inside the parlor and nodded a good evening to Sherman Cooper, who was sitting in an old leather chair.

"He's out looking for Sally. One minute he's kicking her out of the truck and the next minute he's chasing her all over Maury County. You know Bill."

Sherman Cooper spoke, "Did you see the man who claims to be your half-brother?"

Phillip said, "No. Say, I'd like to have one of what you folks are drinking, now that I'm all grown up."

Amanda said, "I'll fix you a drink."

"Bourbon and water."

Phillip turned his attention to Sherman Cooper when his grandmother had left the room. He said, "Been a big day, ain't it?"

Sally Weeds had changed her mind about going to the bowling alley and decided to get out at the Holiday Inn. She told George Atworth to let her out at the caution light a block below. She didn't want them seen together. George leaned across her to help her find the door handle of the late-model rental car. As he leaned away from the driver's side of the car, a bullet smashed through the windshield and tore through the back of the seat where the black man's head had been a moment earlier. The bullet had come from a vehicle directly in front of them. Sally Weeds was jerked back across the seat as George Atworth slid his foot from the brake and mashed the accelerator. He fishtailed the car down Jackson Road out of the mainstream of traffic. Sally Weeds frantically searched the floorboard of the car for the contents of her spilled purse. The black man craned his neck to keep the road in view through a spider-webbed windshield. Sally screamed at him, "What happened to the car? What's wrong? Where are you going?"

The young man pulled the car to the side of the road on a darkened street. He turned off the lights and looked back to see if they were being followed. There was no traffic. He spoke as quietly as his panic would permit. "Somebody shot at us! Somebody tried to kill me."

Sally screamed again, "Oh, my God! My God! Let me out of here."

She still couldn't find the door handle. She clawed at the passenger's side of the car. George Atworth grabbed her arm in a tight grip. "Listen! Calm down! Listen to me! Don't breathe a word of this. Don't tell anybody this happened. Don't call the police."

"He'll kill me! I know he will! I was afraid he'd see us!"

"Who?"

"Gorman, you fool! Gorman Weeds. My ex! I told you!"

George relaxed his hold on her arm. "Can you walk from here?"

"I can walk. I'm not hurt. I'm okay. I'll see you. Thank you. Bye!" The woman half fell, half stepped from the car. She wrapped her arms around her body and stared around as if lost.

George said, "It's behind you. The Holiday Inn is back there. Keep quiet about this."

"Oh, God!" She ran up the street toward the Holiday Inn.

The black man felt the stream of perspiration from his brow and for an instant thought it was blood. He wiped his hand across his forehead and realized he was not hurt. He drove around Jackson Heights subdivision for a few blocks with his lights off, then found his way back to 31. He saw the road sign that would take him to I-65 north, and he drove on toward Nashville. As he drove cautiously in the right lane of the interstate, he remembered an admonition from his chief in Detroit: "George, I know you want this assignment, but remember—a reporter should report the news, not become news."

Sherman Cooper glanced at his watch and mumbled that he really should be getting back to Nashville. Amanda Zephries was talking on the phone. She sounded concerned about something. "Are you sure you're all right? Phillip is here. You want to talk to him? He might know where Bill went." She hollered into the parlor, "Phillip, would you come and talk to Sally? She's looking for Bill."

Phillip went to the phone. As his grandmother handed him the receiver, he covered the receiver with his hand and said, "I wish these two people would find one another and leave me alone." He spoke into the phone, "Sally, Phillip here. Did Bill find you?"

Sally's voice betrayed her panic. "Phillip, something's happened real bad. You gotta come over here to the Holiday Inn and get me. Come on over right now. I'll be in the ladies' room. Knock on the door. Oh, please hurry!" She started to cry and hung up the phone.

Phillip stood and stared into the mouthpiece. He said, more or less to himself, "What the shit is all this about?"

Amanda spoke loudly from the parlor, "Is she okay? She sounded upset to me."

"Oh, I don't know what the hell's going on. I'm going over there and see what she's into. I'll be back in a while."

"Where is she?"

"Said she would be in the ladies' room at the Holiday Inn. Good night, Sherman. Be careful out there. It's wet."

When Phillip came to Main Street in Spring Hill, he noticed his gas gauge read empty. He turned left and drove up to the self-service gas pumps at Kirk's Bi-Rite. He was filling the tank of the rental car when Gorman Weeds came out of the Spring Hill liquor store. Gorman spotted his old schoolmate and spoke to him in a shy voice. "Hey, Phillip, how you doin'?"

Phillip looked up from the hose nozzle and spoke casually. "I'm out of gas. Other than that I'm doing fair. How about you?"

"I had to take my mama into the Baptist Hospital in Nashville this afternoon. I got her checked in for some kinda test. I reckon she'll be all right though."

Phillip hung the nozzle back on the pump rack. "I'm sorry to hear that. Hope she checks out okay."

Gorman stared at the ground for a second. "Uh, look, Phillip, ain't no bad blood 'tween you and me. I don't like your brother, but that's 'tween me and him. Understand?"

"I understand."

"I been hanging 'round that hospital all evenin', just got back over here and thought I'd have a little toddy. Want one?"

"No thanks, Gorman, I've got to go somewhere right now. Thank you though."

Gorman seemed pleased with the exchange. He walked toward his car and spoke over his shoulder, "Well, take care then. Be seein' you."

"See you."

Phillip looked into his rearview mirror as he pulled away from Kirk's Bi-Rite. He saw Muff and Puff coming around the corner to Gorman's white Plymouth.

He thought of how different they all were, the people who had grown up and gone to school together in Spring Hill. He had gone off to college, read some books, heard some lectures, sat in the oak-paneled rooms of academia, and felt a sense of joy in being learned and liberal. And underneath it all he loved his brother and the carefree vernacular of his language, his casual and practical approach to life. Had he been brainwashed? Was there a realism that he had missed somewhere along the way? Was there a fine line? Or as Sherman Cooper would say, a gray line?

Phillip had had a few drinks. He violently shook his head

from side to side and decided to forget about who he was for awhile.

Why did he care about Gorman? Was it some sort of football alliance? They had been coached to hang together. They had taken their lumps side by side on the field; an alliance like that was hard to break. Maybe Gorman wasn't all bad. But Phillip knew that Gorman Weeds had a lot of problems. Anything that went beyond his immediate desire was considered phony and political. He had no patience with waitresses, bartenders, bosses, women, or temperate men. Phillip wondered how he got that way. Didn't they all grow up in the same county? Didn't they all attend the same schools? Same classes? Same books? Same teachers? Same kind of parents? And that is where it ended. Different blood?

Phillip drove toward Columbia and considered blood. It was not fair to consider blood. How about Bill? And what about George Atworth?

Phillip stood in front of the door to the ladies' rest room at the Holiday Inn. Just as he knocked, a tall, black-haired woman came out. She drew back when she realized it was he who had knocked. "The men's room is down there," she said, pointing down the hall.

Phillip looked embarrassed. "Thank you. Is there a blonde lady in there?"

"Yeah, there is. She's been crying about something. You her friend?"

"Yes. Would you tell her Phillip Zephries is out here, please?" The lady opened the door behind her and hollered into the room. "Hey, there's a guy name of Phil Zephlen here to see you." She let the door close. "She's coming out."

Phillip said, "Zephries."

The woman walked off looking puzzled.

Sally Weeds cracked the door of the rest room, "Oh Lord, Phillip, I'm glad you're here. You seen Bill?"

"No. What happened?"

Sally looked both ways in the hallway. "Let's get out of this place first."

"My car's outside. Let's go."

Sally told the whole story. Phillip listened in fascination, then threw his hands in the air. "This is incredible! I can't get it through my thick skull how small this town is. You say the black guy's name was Atworth?"

"George Atworth. I think I've seen him someplace. He sure seems familiar."

"That's incredible."

Sally Weeds began to regain her composure. "I'm gonna have that damned Gorman locked up. I'm not puttin' up with this from him anymore."

Phillip was quiet for a second. "No, no, it wasn't Gorman. He was with his mama at the hospital tonight. I saw him down at the liquor store."

"Really? Well, who in the hell was it?"

"I don't know. You haven't seen Bill all evening?"

"Uh, what do you mean? No, I haven't seen him. You don't think Bill tried to shoot me, do you? He's crazy, but he's not that crazy."

"No, I didn't say that. Bill wouldn't shoot you. He wouldn't shoot anybody."

"Hey, you're saying they were shooting at that nigger, is that it?"

"Could be. Reporters have to ask a lot of questions. He might have pissed somebody off. Maybe some nut didn't like the idea of a black man and a white woman riding around Columbia, Tennessee, together. Get it?"

"Well, I can see that. But I feel better any way it is. I thought that damned Gorman was trying to kill me."

"Was Atworth hurt?"

"I couldn't tell. I don't think so. He just kept saying keep quiet, keep quiet. That's all he could say. There's a hole in the windshield big as a fifty-cent piece. It was a big gun of some kind, right in front of us. It all happened so fast you couldn't think straight."

Phillip slowed the car as they approached Spring Hill. "Listen, do as the man said. Don't say a word about this to anybody. I might know that Atworth fellow. I'll get in touch with him and see what I can find out. Don't mention this to Bill or anybody. I'll take you home. If anybody asks why I came over to get you and bring you home, just say you were sick. Say you got nauseated and wanted a ride home. Just say you were in the rest room sick, and I came and got you. Whoever fired that shot is long gone by now anyway. Just wait until I get back to you. Okay?"

"Well, it suits me. I don't want to get involved if I don't have to. If they was shootin' at him, it suits the hell outta me. Take me by my trailer . . . I really am gettin' sick."

Next morning Phillip learned that Bill had come in very late. The rest of the family had been asleep when he stumbled in and went straight to his bed.

Til prepared breakfast for Phillip and Amanda at the little breakfast nook in the kitchen. Phillip explained that Sally Weeds had gotten sick at the Holiday Inn and had just wanted a ride home. He made no mention of the violent happening.

Bill Zephries laboriously opened his eyes. They felt glued together. He had a hangover from too much Jack Daniels whiskey and marijuana. He could feel the floating pain in his head. If he lay still and did not move, the pain would be there but inactive. If he moved his head in any direction, the pain would bang against the inside of his skull.

He lay as still as possible and tried to remember the events of the night before. He had gone to Spring Hill to look for Sally. He had sat in the parking lot of the Holiday Inn for an hour or more drinking from a bootleg bottle of Jack Daniels and smoking marijuana, and that's when things began to grow dim in his memory. He could remember slamming his fist into the dash of his pickup. Under the covers of the bed he moved his left hand across the knuckles of his right hand. He could feel the broken skin and the soreness.

This was the sixth or seventh time he had blacked out in the past six months. It frightened him. He cursed Saturn, General Motors, Jack Daniels, and marijuana. Sitting on the side of the bed, his head in his hands, Bill Zephries made himself a promise to quit the booze.

Preacher Joseph Armes had told him in confidence that his father had been a heavy drinker. Scott Zephries had been known to take a quart of whiskey to the fields and woods of the farm and walk and drink until he fell unconscious.

Bill Zephries thought of his father on this morning. He could imagine a sickness so violent and a circumstance so depressing that a man could take his own life, as his father had done.

Bill had been eighteen years old when Preacher Armes had told him about his father. He had been working his tobacco one afternoon when the preacher drove up from out of nowhere and started talking. He had been calm and detached at first. But as the story about Rosanna Zephries's running away and Scott Zephries's suicide unfolded, the fiery-eyed preacher had taken on an evangelical tone of voice. Bill remembered a quotation the man had used: "As the twig is bent the tree will grow!"

Bill had never told Phillip about the run-in with the preacher at the tobacco barn. He thought it best to let his older brother come to his own conclusions.

The long-legged young man sat on the side of the bed, holding his head in his hands, and played his favorite philosophical game, "Add 'em up." What did he want? How could he get it? Who would it hurt?

As he sat there, his head pounding and the nausea rumbling in his stomach, the playing of the game made him feel better. He wanted some of everything life had to offer. He was tired of being a farmer. He could get what he wanted by selling the damned farm. If he got hurt in the process, he would only be hurting himself. Bill Zephries wanted the biggest tobacco warehouse in Tennessee. He believed in keeping things as simple as possible.

But what he wanted at the moment was relief from the sickness that greeted him with the day. He reached far back under his mattress and found a small plastic bag of cocaine. He took a small plastic spoon from his bedside drawer. He scooped a tiny amount of the cocaine into the spoon and sniffed it into his nose. He replaced the bag and the spoon where they had been and lay back to wait for what he called "the best hangover medicine in the world" to take effect.

The small plastic bag of cocaine that lay hidden under Bill Zephrie's mattress was the second such bag he had ever bought.

It was after ten when Bill found his way down the stairs. He was starting to feel better already. He saw Phillip sitting at the small kitchen table. "Mornin'. Is that coffee fresh?"

Phillip moved his chair back from the table a little distance. "Til made it a few minutes ago."

"Where is she?"

"She's cleaning somewhere in the house. Amanda went to the post office. What's wrong with your eyes?"

"Well, a strange thing happened last night. I couldn't find Sally, so I went over to Nashville to check out the action and somebody started putting liquor in my drinks. Ever have a thing like that happen to you?" Bill poured himself a cup of black coffee.

Phillip sipped his coffee. "I've heard that Nashville is an evil old town."

"It is. Oh, it damned sure is. Say, did you hear from Sally last night?"

"Yeah, well, she called me from the Holiday Inn and wanted me to come and get her. She was sick at her stomach. Said she was looking for you."

"Hmmnn, how'd she get to Columbia?"

"I don't know. Caught a ride, I guess."

"I told you that was her in that car we passed. Where in hell did she go? I checked two or three places before I went over to Nashville."

"I don't know."

Bill finished the cup of coffee and sat it on the table. He went to stand by the kitchen window that looked out to where his father was buried. "Wonder what the old man would have thought of your mama marrying a nigger."

Phillip's face became grim. "If you're looking for someone to hang a guilt trip on about that, I'm not the place to start."

"Well, seems to me you don't seem to be all that upset about it."

"How in the hell would you go about changing it now?"

Bill lit a cigarette and blew the smoke toward the ceiling. "Well, now, son, there's ways to change things."

Phillip said, "Like killing a few people?"

"I just said there's ways to change things."

Phillip saw the chance to pursue his conversational inquiry. "You didn't by any chance drive through Columbia early last evening, did you?"

Bill seemed confused by the question. "Yeah, I told you I was going back to look for Sally."

"Didn't happen to see George Atworth, did you?"

"Naw, the gal at the desk said he checked out yesterday afternoon. Good thing I didn't see the son of a bitch. I was pissed enough to kick his ass."

Phillip looked carefully at his brother. He knew Bill was not a good liar and sensed that he didn't know he was being interrogated.

Til came into the room wiping her hands on her apron and looking sternly at the two men. "You boys ain't fightin' already, are you? I hear these voices gettin' louder and louder, jes like the ol' days."

Bill said, "Til, has Amanda told you that we've heard something about our mother?"

Til's eyebrows raised. "No, she sho ain't tole me nothin' like that."

"Well, get her to tell you about it."

Til said, "Why don't you tell?"

"I don't want to."

"Why don't you tell, Phillip?"

Phillip stood to leave the room. He spoke over his shoulder, leering at Bill. "My big brother doesn't want me to."

Bill said, "Til, how 'bout ironing that blue cowboy shirt for me? I'm going up to get a shower."

When both men had left the room, Til shouted after them, "I guess I'll read 'bout it in the paper."

Til ironed the worn blue cowboy shirt. As she ironed she heard the shower running. She put the shirt on a hanger and took it upstairs. When she reached Bill's room, she quietly said, "Hoo hoo?" There was no reply to the familiar sound. She quietly opened the door to the room and saw Bill lying stretched across the bed asleep. He was wearing a pair of faded bluejeans, no socks, and no shirt. She hung the shirt on the doorknob and went back downstairs.

Phillip was in the parlor. Til asked him if he needed anything. He looked up from his reading and said, "Til, does Bill keep his hunting rifle on that rack in his truck all the time?"

Til looked at the far wall as if trying to remember. "Far as I know he does. He ain't shot nobody, has he?" Til laughed.

"I don't think so. I was out in the yard a few minutes ago, and his gun's not there now."

"Sometimes he keep it in the closet upstairs. It depends."

"On what?"

Til shook her head in bewilderment. "Lawd, I don't know, I don't go huntin'. What you need a gun fo'?"

"I don't need a gun. Forget it."

Til sat down on the edge of a chair, leaned forward, and spoke quietly. "Tell 'bout yo' mama. Tell me."

Phillip laid his book aside. "Til, our mama, when she moved to Detroit, married a black man." He looked the black woman in the eye waiting for a reply.

Til sat bolt upright in her chair. "What'd she do dat fo'?"

"Who knows?"

"She married a black man?"

"He was a doctor."

"A people doctor?"

"Yes."

"Lawd, Lawd."

Phillip said, "Look, Til, we didn't mention it before because we didn't want to hurt your feelings. Bill's really upset about it. They had a son, and he came down here yesterday. He's our half-brother and he's black."

"Black as me?"

"Black as you."

"I'd like to have a word with dat boy."

I think he's gone back to Detroit. He's a reporter for a news syndicate there."

"Sweet Jesus! I knew they had some fancy colored folks in Detroit, but I never thought we'd see 'em down here. Did you? What did he want with us?"

"We don't know really; he was just down here on assignment, or so he said."

"Mighty Moses, dis car factory gonna cause more trouble'n Lawd will allow. You watch my word."

"Well, anyway, that's the story, and I thought you should know."

"What's his name?"

"George Atworth."

Til's eyes lit up. "Uh huh, now I see why dat name upset yo' grandmama so. Lawd, Lawd."

"What time is she coming back?"

Til ignored the question. "Does yo' grandmama know I know?"

"Tell her you know."

Til got up to leave the room. "I ain't tellin' yo' grandmama nothin'. She'll get to tellin' sooner or later. Where's Rosanna got to now?"

"I don't know, but the doctor's dead."

"My goodness, what could kill a doctor?"

"It was a car accident."

"Lawd, Lawd, reckon when is all dis gonna stop?"

A few minutes later the phone rang. It was Sally Weeds, and Phillip talked to her. She seemed calmed from the night before and asked Phillip to have Bill call her when he was awake.

When Amanda returned to the Old Zephries Place, she and Til talked a long while in Amanda's room. Dinner was a quiet affair. No one seemed to want to bring up the serious subjects of the past few days. Bill ate slowly and sparingly and said that he was going to pick up Sally and ride around a while. Phillip announced that he was returning to St. Louis the next day. There were polite protests to his sudden announcement, but he insisted that he must clear up a few matters there and then would try to arrange a quick return.

After dinner, Til stood by the sink washing dishes. She said to no one in particular, "I think I gonna see the doctor tomorrow. My blood gettin' up."

CHAPTER FIVE

THEM ZEPHRIES BOYS IS MAKIN' A KILLIN'

Bill Zephries stuck his head into his brother's bedroom and yelled, "I got to go to work, cowboy. Have a good trip and hurry on home."

Phillip mumbled a thank you and picked up his glasses and his watch from the bedside table. It was six-thirty in the morning. He knew it was very cold outside. He could sense the cold even though the room was warm. He put on his pants and his shirt and tiptoed downstairs toward the kitchen, where he could smell breakfast cooking.

Til sat at the little kitchen table drinking coffee. An open Bible lay on the table. She spoke softly. "Mornin'. Did we wake you up?"

"Bill stopped in to say good-bye." Phillip looked around the room, stretched, and yawned. "Do you always get up this early around here?"

"When Bill workin' de tobacco, he get up early. Other times he sleep all day. It depends. You want some coffee?"

"Yes, please."

Til poured the coffee and sat it in front of the young man. She retrieved the Bible from the table, closed it, and placed it on a shelf by the refrigerator.

Phillip said, "Do you read your Bible every morning?"

"I read it most mornin's as usual. Mornin' ain't no time

for black folks. We night people."

"Is that true?"

"It's true if you pore and black."

"Well, you might like to know that mornings are no good for white folks either." Phillip wiped his glasses on a paper towel. "Til, what do the folks you talk to think of the Saturn plant coming here?"

The black woman stood by the sink and sipped a cup of coffee. She put her elbows on the kitchen counter and looked out the window. She spoke to the window as if she had rehearsed her speech. "Well, now, I think most black folks are fo' it. Some folks say dey gonna tear up de grass and trees when dey come here. Black folks so pore dey ain't got time to look at trees and grass. Dey want some jobs. Anytime folks get ready to build somethin' roun' here dey just tear up what dey please. Grass, trees, graveyards, and anything else dat get in de way; don't make no difference. Dey leave all dey junk and lumber and stuff piled up any old which way as long as dey get built what dey buildin'. Now, these car folks comin' in and say dey gonna look after things and keep it neat. We never heard no neat talk 'til dey come in. See what I mean?"

"I see what you mean."

Til turned from the counter and looked at the young man. She spoke firmly. "Boy, I ain't worried 'bout them car folks comin' down here. I'se worried 'bout you boys and yo' grand-mama. She too old and nervy to be worryin' herself sick over all dis. You better pay attention to yo' grandmama. She might up and die on you over somethin' like dis. Folks think 'cause dey live a long time dey gonna live forever. Dey ain't but two red lights in Spring Hill, and if dey come down here and put in twenty-five mo', it ain't gonna make yo' grandmama any younger."

Phillip crossed his legs and took his bare foot in his hand. "You know, Til, I think there's something about all of this in that Bible of yours. It sounds crazy to a lot of people, but why are we selling this place? Greed. It's simple. If someone had come along with an offer when this land was five hundred dollars an acre, we would have treated him like a traveling salesman. It never crossed our minds to sell this place before Saturn. Now, it's the prostitute and the money story. Remember that? A man asked a woman if she would sleep with a stranger for a million dollars, and she said she probably would. He asked her if she would sleep with a stranger for ten dollars, and she wanted to know what kind of woman he thought she was. He said he knew what kind of woman she was, he was just negotiating a price."

Til looked at him in mock anger. "Listen, boy, dat story ain't in my Bible."

TWA flight 247 roared into the skies of middle Tennessee at 10:26 that morning, away from Spring Hill. Phillip Zephries, seated by a window, peered down at the frosty landscape looking for the three hundred acres of land that would make him a millionaire. He sipped the coffee the stewardess had brought him and scanned through the *Columbia Herald* newspaper for any word of the Saturn Project. There was a piece about the Columbia Dam project that said the dam would probably not be completed, even with the coming of Saturn. TVA had already spent eighty million dollars on the fifty million dollar project, and it was only forty-five percent complete. Phillip ran the numbers through his mind as the aircraft made its way to St. Louis. They made as little sense as three million dollars for fallow farm land.

Phillip Zephries had rented a one-bedroom apartment in a high-rise three blocks from where he worked. As the cab driver got his bags from the trunk, Phillip looked down the street to his office building. He watched the young, energetic people coming and going and was tempted to go straight to his office himself, but he dismissed the urge and caught the elevator to his sixth-floor apartment. He adjusted the heat in his carefully decorated apartment and switched on the audiotape device of the telephone. He sat on a large, plush, beige-colored sofa and listened to the recorded messages:

"Phillip, this is Alicia. Call me when you get back from the wilds of Tennessee and we'll paarrty!"

"Zephries, Red here. Listen, we need a color change on the tomato can for Rogers. He says he wants it to look American. You know, red against white, and some blue on the thing. I know you're on vacation, I know, I know, but this guy has been praying about this thing. If we don't get to the conservative son of a bitch before God does, we're gonna lose the account. For Christ's sake, I know you can dabble in red, white, and blue. I know you're checking your messages . . . Call me right away."

"Mister Zephries, this is the service department at Ford. Your car needs a new water pump. We can't do the work without authorization from you. Please call us as soon as possible. Thank you."

"Phillip, this is Susan. You left your dirty gym suit in my car. If you don't come get it, I'm going to bury it in my back yard. We had a date for—"

Phillip switched off the machine and called his office. He got the switchboard and asked for Red Ottery. A girl answered the ring. "Phil, this is Alicia. Red's out. Did you get his message about Rogers?"

"Yes."

"Can you come in for a few minutes?"

"Not right away. I'm into something a little heavy. It's going okay, but if I get into the office right now it'll ruin my week. I want to settle this thing before I get back to work."

"I can understand that."

"Don't you think Jim can handle that Rogers tomato can thing? To tell you the truth, I'm sick of the project and had hoped it'd be gone before I got back."

"I think Jim can do it, but Red wanted me to find you."

"Tell him you couldn't reach me."

"I'll do it. You'll owe me one."

"I owe you one. Bye!"

Phillip rubbed the back of his stiff neck with his hand. He stretched and looked around the room. It had been decorated by a girlfriend who had wanted to use it as a showpiece for potential clients. She had shown the place only one time before moving back to Philadelphia with verbal scorn for the hokey taste of the people of St. Louis.

Phillip dialed information in Detroit, Michigan. "Commocorp Corporation, please." He wrote the number down and dialed the 313 area code and the number. A woman's voice answered. Phillip said, "Mister George Atworth, please."

"What department?"

"He's a reporter."

"One moment."

As the phone buzzed somewhere in the Commocorp complex, Phillip wondered at the absence of the word *please* from the switchboard. He mused that it sounded like an all-business operation. A male voice came over the phone. "Yeah!"

"George Atworth, please."

"Hang on a sec. George, phone, line two."

"Atworth here."

Phillip stared at the mouthpiece. In his haste to make the call, he had not thought through his approach to this strange

89

but related man. "Uh, George, this is Phillip. Phillip Zephries."

"Where are you?"

"St. Louis."

"Hang on, I want to take this in private."

There were a few seconds of silence. Then George Atworth spoke. "Why are you calling me? What do you want?"

"I want to talk about what happened to you and Sally Weeds."

Another few moments of silence. "Hey, how'd you hear about that?"

"It's a little hard to explain, and it might be harder to believe."

George coughed nervously into the phone. "Shoot."

"Sally Weeds, the girl you talked to, she's my brother Bill's girlfriend."

George Atworth said flatly, "Your brother's girlfriend."

"Right."

Phillip began to think he was sounding silly. "Look, Spring Hill is a small town with a capital small."

"Go on."

"She told me the story. I want you to know that it had nothing to do with family. We're not that kind of people."

"Then it didn't make the news?"

"No."

"Good. Got any idea who could have done it? The girl said it was her ex." George Atworth sounded like a reporter.

Phillip backed off. "Hey, you're not writing about it, are you?"

"No, no! Hell no! I just want to know who would like to have me dead."

"It was not her ex, my brother, me, or anything of that sort."

"I didn't say that."

"I know you didn't. But the whole damned thing was

coming down so quickly. The week was a bitch, all of it."

"You should have been in the car."

"I'm sorry about it. I guess that's what I want to say."

"Okay, okay, let's say I believe you. Let's say some redneck just took a shot at a black guy and a white woman. Is that the way you want to leave it?"

"I don't know. I don't have an answer. But I want to check around. It's for damned sure somebody, somewhere, knows what happened. If I find out anything, I'll let you know. Fair enough?"

"What makes you think I want to know? I don't really give a damn. I'm through in Spring Hill. I'm home now with other things to do. I just delivered my mother's message."

Phillip hesitated, then said, "We're brothers whether we like it or not. I don't know how you feel, but I don't know why we couldn't be friends."

The phone was silent for a moment. George Atworth spoke firmly. "Let me give you my home number. If you need to call me, call me there."

Phillip wrote the number down. "I'll call you if it's important."

Sally Weeds strolled the aisles of what the proprietors cleverly called "The Grocery Store." She carried a roll of paper towels, a jar of instant coffee, and a carton of cigarettes in her arms as she spotted her former mother-in-law. She walked toward the white-haired woman and said in her kindest voice, "Ethel, how are you feeling?"

"Oh, hi, Sally. I guess I'm feeling all right. A little arthritis

I've always had, but nothing serious, I reckon. How are you doin', honey?"

"I'm lookin' for a job if you hear of anything."

"Well, you know I don't get out much to hear of nothing like that. Is Gorman leavin' you alone?"

"Not much."

"I worry 'bout that boy day and night. He done you wrong, honey. You tried to make a home for him. I know that. Lord knows something's gonna kill us all, but I expect to hear any night that he's got hisself killed or killed somebody. He won't stop drinking and runnin' with them Brannigan boys. They're a rough bunch. I ain't seen him in two or three weeks."

Sally Weeds glared. "You haven't seen him in weeks?"

"No, I don't reckon he cares what happens to me —"

"He said he took you to the Nashville hospital just the other night."

"Lord, he ain't took me no place. And I sure wouldn't go all the way to Nashville to no hospital. My doctors are at Williamson County. Always have been. They took out my gall-bladder that time."

Sally Weeds caught her breath. "You mean Gorman didn't take you to the hospital?"

"Why, honey, I told you I ain't seen him in almost a month, didn't I?"

Sally said, "Yes, yes, you did. Ethel, I gotta run. You take care of yourself, you hear?"

"Okay, honey, come see me now. Promise you will."

"I will, I will." Sally Weeds walked toward the front of the store. She muttered under her breath, "That son of a bitch tried to kill me."

Bill Zephries was the talk of Spring Hill, Tennessee, for the winter of 1985 and the early spring of 1986. He drove a new Cadillac, wore clothes that bore strange name tags, and spent most of his time in the more modern clubs of Nashville.

Sally Weeds, silent about her knowledge of Gorman Weeds's alibi on the night of the shooting, accepted the gift of a used Chevrolet Camaro automobile from the playboy Bill Zephries and took a job showing real estate to the still swarming speculators in the area. She moaned about the new girlfriends and the new lifestyle of the once-country boyfriend Zephries.

Phillip Zephries did not come home for Christmas. He sent cards and modest gifts. Bill, on the other hand, lavished gifts on almost everyone, and especially on Amanda Zephries and Til.

The winter and spring brought news of Saturn. On January 16 it was said that natural gas would be coming to Spring Hill.

On January 17 it was announced that a group called Representatives for Responsible Growth had been formed in the area.

On January 26 it was learned that someone wanted to do a video presentation for newcomers to Maury County. On that same date it was reported that Marvin Wright, when asked about Saturn, said, "We don't need that plant. What we need is a good rain."

In early December, Laurie Kay became the Saturn spokesman.

On December 9, Gorman Weeds was arrested for driving under the influence of alcohol.

On February 2 of '86, Sally Weeds complained that her water bill had gone up along with every other water bill in Spring Hill.

On February 7, there was a notice that Saturn had a mailing address and a telephone number. It was:

Saturn Corp.
P.O. Box 488
Highway 31 South
Spring Hill, Tenn. 37174
Phone 615-486-5000

On April Fools' Day of the spring of '86, Phillip Zephries took one look back into the empty apartment where he had lived for the past few years. A trailer hitched to the back of his car held all of his possessions. He was on his way back to Spring Hill and the fortune that awaited him there. He had been coaxed back by the insistent demands of both Amanda Zephries and Sherman Cooper. Bill Zephries was having a high old time on the prospect of the money to come, and the two elders wanted Phillip at home.

In Spring Hill, Tennessee, at the Saturn site, a bluebird entered a hollowed fence post with a tiny piece of straw in its beak. Sunlight bathed the Saturn site, and water from a recent shower trickled merrily down Carters Creek.

Life rolled on at the Old Zephries Place. Til washed linen for the bed of Phillip Zephries, who would arrive late in the evening.

Bill Zephries was in Nashville looking for cocaine. Word was around that the police were planning a general bust. He had already tried two reliable sources and could not find his dealer. He pulled into the parking lot of a large office building, turned off the ignition to kill the motor, and then turned it back on to keep the radio playing. A small, dark youth stopped by the window of his car, leaned in, and said, "Hey man, got a match? Oh, it's John Wayne." The dealers had given Bill Zephries the name because of his height and his habit of wearing cowboy boots. "Hang on, Duke!"

The young man went into an alleyway and was gone a few seconds before a taller, older man appeared at the window of the Cadillac. Bill Zephries handed the man a hundred dollar bill.

The man placed a small packet in his hand. Zephries said, "Ain't these things getting smaller?" The man looked around the parking area, then leaned his head farther into the window. "Ah, man, the more you boogie the smaller they get." The man glanced around the area again. He spoke quietly. "You want a bargain, I can get it for you, but you gotta buy a ton. You want a ton?"

Bill Zephries said, "How much?"

The man scribbled a telephone number on a soiled piece of paper and said, "Here, call this number and ask for Bobby. Tell him Gabby sent you."

Then the man was gone.

Bill Zephries drove out of the parking lot wondering what the man meant by a ton.

Til and Amanda sat on the back steps of the Old Zephries Place drinking coffee. They watched the bee-like activity of several young men clad in blue coveralls milling about on the landscape of the farm.

Til had found Amanda upstairs that morning and had announced that there was a group of Chinese people swarming all over the farm. Amanda had assured her that they were Japanese and that they were there to appraise the property. Til had said, "You mean we gonna sell this place to a bunch of Jap people?"

Amanda had explained that Sherman Cooper had said their money was as good as anybody's.

The two women sat with their knees pulled toward their stomachs and their arms folded around them. Amanda said, in a sort of whisper, "The Japanese are a very thorough people. They want to know the mineral content of the land, the water-shed, the value of the lumber and everything."

Til made a scoffing sound. "We never did know all dat, did we?"

"I don't suppose we needed to know. Is your coffee still hot?"

"No, it got cold. I'll get us a cup. You 'spose we oughta offer some to dem little Jap boys?"

"They're not boys, Til, they're grown men. They are very small people."

Til spoke as she entered the kitchen door, "Well, no wonder we whooped 'em in the war den."

Amanda heard a car at the front of the house. She was expecting Sherman Cooper, so she hollered into the kitchen where Til was making coffee, "Til, tell Mister Cooper to come around back. And pour some coffee for him."

Sherman Cooper came around the side of the house brushing twigs from his trouser leg. "Mornin', Amanda. Beautiful day, isn't it?"

"Hi, Sherman. Lord, it sure is. I'm so tired of winter."

"Bill hasn't been doing much yard work out here, has he?" Amanda patted the porch step with her hand. "Have a seat. No, Bill hasn't started that tractor in over a month. I guess he's out of the farming business for good. I used to love the sound of the tractor going around the property. It had a nice secure hum to it. Know what I mean?"

"Absolutely. I like the sound myself."

Amanda said, "I don't know what's got into Bill. One minute he's happy as a lark and next minute he's brooding."

Til leaned from the kitchen door and handed Amanda two cups of coffee. "Mister Cooper? You take cream and sugar, sir?"

"No, thank you, Til. I'm watching my weight."

Til mumbled as she closed the screen door to the kitchen, "Don't see why old folks care what dey weigh. When old black folks is skinny, dey more'n likely sick."

Sherman Cooper sipped his coffee and loosened his tie. He glanced back at the kitchen door and said, "I've often wondered why Til doesn't speak English if she can speak English."

Amanda laughed, "She's like all the other people around here. They can speak any old way they please. It just depends on who they're talking to and what they're trying to say. It amazes me too."

The two old friends sat in silence for a few minutes watching the workers collect soil samples, rocks, and snips of vegetation. One young man used a complicated device to measure and grade trees. Off in the distance there was the sound of a portable drill getting core samples of rock and subsoil.

Amanda stretched her arms in the air and took a deep breath of fresh, country air. She put her hand on Sherman's shoulder. "Is this the last step?"

"I can't think of anything else. If this is all analyzed in the next week or so, the deal is final."

"I sure would be disappointed if they discovered gold or oil and didn't tell us about it," Amanda laughed.

The silver-haired man smiled. "You know, Amanda, there was a time when a Maury County farmer could walk across this farm in thirty minutes and tell you exactly what these young scientists will know in two weeks."

"What do you suppose they'll do with the land?"

"I have no idea."

"I guess it doesn't matter now."

"As best I know, it's speculation. Just real estate investment."

"The money is secure, isn't it?"

"This firm is solid as a rock. If they don't pay us, we can confiscate about half of San Francisco." Sherman Cooper laughed.

Amanda turned to her friend and spoke in earnest. "Sherman, what do you really think of all this Saturn business?"

The quiet-spoken man said, "Just that. What you said. Business. There will always be construction and destruction in business. Things aren't made to last anymore. We tear down almost as much as we build. Technology demands adventurous thinking in corporate minds. We really need to retool our entire steel industry. We need to take long, hard looks at our automobile industry, as GM is doing here. It can change almost overnight. We've come so far technologically; it's difficult to get a product to the consumer before it's obsolete. Parts and services are in a terrible trap right now. Industry wishes the consumer would just run some of these things off a cliff into the ocean and start all over. Saturn and its satellites will put three million dollars a week into the economy of Maury County. No harm can come from that. We are a capitalistic society. Much of this money will wind up in churches, schools, nursing homes, hospitals, and in the hands of local governments. Most of the growth will be so gradual no one will much notice, unless he or she stays under the bed for a few years. Of course, there are people who will do that." The lawyer brushed his trouser leg and smiled.

"Did you ask them how long I can stay here?"

"Yes, I did. I don't think there's a problem at all. They're not interested in the house. I have to draw up a little paper releasing them from liability. These people have a very high regard for the elderly, if you don't mind me saying so, and they understand your feelings entirely. They've offered thirty days' notice. That pleased me. I've grown fond of them through these negotiations."

Amanda stretched her arms and yawned slightly. "Oh, it's so peaceful here." Her voice took a more serious tone as she said, "I'll have to move the remains of Gyp and Scott, won't I?"

Sherman put his arm around the woman. "You know how I feel about bridges, Amanda. That's a decision we don't have to make today. When the time comes, you'll do the right thing. I know it."

"I've thought and prayed about it."

"Good."

There was a sound of automobile tires on gravel. Bill Zephries's Cadillac rounded the drive onto the farm road at the back of the house. Amanda waved, Sherman Cooper stood and straightened his tie. Bill got out from the car and reached his hand out for a young woman who had exited the passenger side. "Hi, y'all. Howdy, Sherman."

"Hello, Bill."

Bill turned to the thin young lady at his side. She was dressed in a Neiman Marcus T-shirt, jeans that fitted tightly around her ankles, pale blue sneakers, and she carried a pack of cigarettes and a lighter in her hand. Her light brown hair fell loosely to her shoulders from a casual part in the center of her head. She wore little color on her thin lips, and her high cheekbones under green eyes seemed to be colored by the effects of the spring sun. Bill held his right hand toward her and said, "Linda, you know Amanda, and this is Sherman Cooper. He's an old friend and a lawyer. Sherman, this is my girlfriend, Linda Vanstadt."

Sherman stood and bowed slightly. "How do you do?"

Linda said, "Hi, I believe you know my grandfather."

The lawyer raised his eyebrows. "Judge Vanstadt? Why, yes. He was doing some postgraduate work at Vanderbilt when I was a freshman there."

Amanda Zephries got Bill's attention. "Bill, come with me for a minute, please, something I want to tell you. Will you two excuse us for a minute, please?"

The old lawyer and the young lady nodded.

Linda Vanstadt stood with her hands on her hips appraising Sherman Cooper. "My grandfather has spoken of you often."

"Oh, really, I'm flattered. How is he? I heard about the stroke." The young lady sat down on the steps. Sherman Cooper joined her. "He's doing as well as can be expected at his age. He sits on the veranda at Belle Meade Country Club and watches the golfers. It seems to be his favorite pastime."

"I would think so. He was a seven handicapper at one time."

"Well, I know very little about the game."

"Did you go to Vanderbilt?"

"Yes, American history major."

"Graduate?"

"Oh, yes. It would have been scandalous not to."

"What was your thesis?"

"I'm surprised you'd care."

"I'm fascinated by history. I would have preferred it, but I came from a legal family. You know how that goes."

"Yes, well, it was 'The Myth Of Morality In Early Twentieth Century America.'"

"Lively subject."

"Isn't it, though." Linda Vanstadt squinted her eyes at Sherman Cooper. "You know, Maury County has an interesting history. This territory was once known as Washington District, North Carolina. It was organized in 1784 and was named for George Washington. The Cherokee Indians had title to it for a long time, but it doesn't take an historian to know what happened to the Indians. The war department directed Captain Samuel Butler to cut the Natchez Trace through this territory to get to the Mississippi River. Maury wasn't even a county then."

Sherman Cooper said, "Hmmmm, how did Spring Hill get its name?"

Linda continued, "There are over forty small spring-fed streams that feed the Duck River. Columbia was built around Burns Spring. Many of these springs are called 'never-failing' springs. And Spring Hill got its name from those famous springs." Linda laughed, "Forgive me for being familiar, but speaking of more recent history, wasn't there a slight to-do about you and Missus Zephries some years ago?"

Sherman Cooper blanched for a second, then laughed. "Well, Miss, I'll tell you. I was happily married to the same woman for over thirty years, rest her soul. Missus Zephries and I are, and have been, family friends. I did legal work for her late husband as a young lawyer. And I might add that I'm disappointed in Judge Vanstadt. Rumor often rewrites history."

Linda Vanstadt smiled broadly. "I think the disappointment is mutual. The judge always said that you had more potential than ambition."

"Oh, he did, did he? Well, I'll have to go by the veranda one day and reprimand him."

"I'm sure he'd love to see you."

Sherman Cooper's face could not hide his interest in the unusual young lady at his side. He stared off into the trees of the farm as he spoke casually. "Since we're being candid, I find you and Bill Zephries a rather odd couple."

Linda Vanstadt's voice became defensive. "Mister Cooper, I hate tea, detest tennis, abhor bridge, and simply cannot stomach sushi. That eliminates me as a social success at Belle Meade. I find Bill Zephries to be a handsome devil and a phenomenal cultural study. Am I being unfair, or just honest?"

The white-maned lawyer coughed slightly. "Well, Miss, you're certainly not short on honesty."

Bill Zephries came back to the door of the kitchen. "Amanda wants me to take her on an errand, as she says. Will you all be okay here for a few minutes?"

Sherman Cooper stood quickly. "I have to be getting back to the office. Tell Amanda I'll be there if she needs me." He turned to Linda Vanstadt, "Tell your grandfather hello for me. I enjoyed meeting you."

"You too, Mr. Cooper," she said. "But before you go, are you and Amanda aware that this house is practically a warehouse of antique furniture?"

"I'm very much aware of that. But I'm afraid Amanda considers it so much furniture."

Linda said, "Oh, well, I just hope she'll let me identify and catalogue some of it." The girl stood and shook his hand. "Do take care."

"Thank you. Good-bye now."

Linda Vanstadt's father and mother had divorced when she was a young girl. It had all been very messy and bitter. She had learned that her father was bisexual and that her mother had shown little or no interest in sex of any kind. Her father preferred Los Angeles to Nashville, and her mother, who had been a botany major, had gotten a minor, though prestigious, position with the Metropolitan Museum of Natural History. Linda Vanstadt had been brought up by her grandfather and grandmother who were bright, happy people who could not conceive of a life outside Belle Meade, Nashville's old money district. She had not been spared the details of her parent's difficulties in marriage, and this brought out in her a sense of straightforwardness that amused her grandfather to loud laughter and approval. He would often use her nickname in saying, "Give 'em hell, Spitz."

Although it was hard to be a social oddity in a town that thrived on such people, Linda Vanstadt had certainly made a name for herself in Nashville. She had met none of the criteria for young ladies of her set. She had had live-in boyfriends of whom she had grown tired. She had traveled abroad with the simple explanation that she wanted a mind's eye view of geography and history. She had wondered long among the ancient ruins in Greece, and she had walked for miles in Rome, trying to see it as Henry James's Daisy Miller had seen it. She shopped in Paris and labored over the long seven-course dinners that were the tradition there. She had tried her French and German to find that she was largely ignored by waiters and shop clerks who could manage a third as much English.

When it was learned that she was going abroad, she had been surprised at the number of Tennesseans living and working there. Letters of introduction went out to a number of international acquaintances of the Nashville community. Since she would be a young lady traveling alone and abroad for the first time, it was recommended that friends living there find her suitable and reputable escorts. There were exchange students she had met at Vanderbilt that she had kept in touch

103

with and would call upon from her own private list. And so she was seldom bored. She would no sooner check into her hotel when the messages would be waiting or start coming in. Her only disappointment was an invitation to tour Paris at night. When she entered the lobby of the hotel to meet her hosts, she found that she was part of a bus tour that included a group of camera-clicking and noisy Japanese. She returned to her room and had a quiet dinner from room service and struggled with a recently purchased book of French poetry.

Next morning in the lobby, she learned that anyone could make the tour for $49 American. She never called her hosts to thank them for the tour.

On returning from the trip abroad, she took a job as a teller in a branch bank of First American. She had often wondered how it would be to meet the public and be a part of the general work force. Her grandfather had objected to such menial work and fussed until she agreed to do postgraduate work at Vanderbilt. She attended a few classes in interior design and twentieth-century architecture before dropping out. It was shortly afterwards that she met Bill Zephries. On that chance meeting, she decided that she had arrived at a new stage of her life.

Linda Vanstadt harbored a vague notion that she had been disadvantaged by the sexual revolution, in which she had become a young woman. She had slept with most of the men that she would have conceivably married in another era. History had taught her that daring, adventurous women were the most interesting and led the most exciting lives.

When she met Bill Zephries at what young people called a "meat market" night club in Nashville, she had been struck by his honesty and his magnificent looks. She had noticed that he had a "real" suntan, not one of those booth tans that were so popular among the usual social set. She summed him up as being a novel of society. She smiled within when she made mental note that once in bed with clothes off, it didn't matter if one could play chess.

Sherman Cooper's Cadillac smelled musty after the time he had spent sitting in the fresh country air. He rolled the windows down a few inches and let the air circulate. His mind went back to the way Bill Zephries was dressed. The young tobacco farmer had turned into a preppie. He had worn baggy brown slacks with pleats in front, a permanently wrinkled, white cotton shirt open at the collar, shoes with a greenish tint to them, and a gold chain around his neck. His hair had been styled, rather than cut, and a small twist of long hair ran down the back of his neck over his shirt collar. Sherman had not mentioned it to Amanda, but he was concerned about Bill Zephries's mood swings; it sounded like a potential drug problem. The old lawyer removed his glasses and rubbed his eyes. A mild depression seemed to come over him. He shook his head to bring his attention back to his driving and muttered the words of the current Spring Hill table talk: "Them Zephries boys is makin' a killin'," he mused. "And maybe getting high."

With Bill and Amanda on an errand and Sherman Cooper gone, Til and Linda Vanstadt were alone in the house.

Linda came into the kitchen where Til was washing coffee cups. The young lady placed her hands on the kitchen counter behind her, jumped lightly, and was seated on the counter with her legs dangling. She watched as Til wiped the coffee cups and placed them in the cupboard.

For a reason she could not verbalize, Til liked Linda Vanstadt. She had an open, honest, sometimes startling view of race relations and morals that Til found oddly exciting.

Linda Vanstadt lit a cigarette and spoke. "Til, how's your love life these days?"

Til laughed nervously. "Ain't none of yo' business 'bout my life on no account."

"What'd you do with that young buck who was up there painting Phillip's room a few days ago?"

"I ain't done nothin' wid him."

"Seems to me you were trying to drown him in lemonade."

Til wiped the kitchen sink furiously. "I give you lemonade same as I did him."

"Yeah, but he didn't walk around staring at my ass all day."

"I cain't help what he starin' at one way or 'nother."

"He was staring at your black ass all day and you liked it."

"Shut yo' mouf, girl. I never heard no lady talk like you in my life. If you wuz my daughter I'd wash yo' mouf wid soap."

"I ain't no lady and you know it. I'm rich, I'm spoiled, and I'm hanging around Bill Zephries so I can be more spoiled and more rich. Is that the story going around?"

"It ain't up to me to know nothin' 'bout what stories is goin' 'round."

Linda extinguished her cigarette in an ashtray. "Tell me about this kept woman Bill's got out here in Spring Hill. What's she look like?"

Til stared at the slim young woman sitting on the counter. "Well, she got some meat on her bones."

Linda raised her eyebrows, "Fat?"

"I didn't say she wuz fat."

"Oh . . . Meat on her bones! Boobs, hey?"

"I don't see how she keep from fallin' down." Til began to giggle uncontrollably.

Linda jumped to the kitchen floor. She placed her hands in her back pockets and walked around the kitchen. She turned and pointed her finger at Til. "What's she think of me?"

Til wiped her hands on the dish towel she was holding. She looked Linda Vanstadt in the eye. "What you think she think? She don't like it. But she got that nice car outta the deal, and she know Bill take it from her if she get huffy. She actin' like she don't know 'bout you rite now. But she thinkin', I know dat much. She thinkin' on it."

"You make it sound as if she were dangerous or something."

Til lowered her eyes and spoke solemnly. "Sally Weeds is a mean country girl. She ain't gonna lay down and cry 'bout it, but she can do somethin' she got a mind to. I'd watch her close if I wuz you. She all time thinkin' on it. She say you makin' a sissy outta Bill. He ain't wore his jeans since I wash and iron 'em two months ago. He gettin' so fat I doubt he be able to get in 'em anyway."

Linda threw up her hands, "Oh, bull! Is that what you think, or is that what Sally big tits thinks? If a man has money he doesn't need to go around dressed like a damned tobacco farmer. I think he looks cute. It's the way young men are dressing these days. And I'm teaching him some manners, too."

Til shrugged her shoulders. "If you ask me, somebody oughta teach you some manners. All that nasty talk in my kitchen. I never heard no such."

"Bullshit! Black people practically invented bad language in America."

Til spoke as she walked toward the parlor door. "And you a college girl and all. I never seen nobody be so sweet and so mannish on the same sunrise. Go out there and get Phillip's sheets off the line and bring 'em upstairs. He like 'em dried in the sun."

"Yes ma'am, I gonna do like you say. I gonna fetch them sheets 'fore the Klan gets 'em and burns down the house. We gonna be good niggers. Good 'uns!"

CHAPTER SIX

THIRTY DAYS' NOTICE

Phillip Zephries was tired and red-eyed when he drove his dusty Ford compact automobile into the parking area behind the Old Zephries Place. It was four-thirty in the afternoon, and the seven-hour drive had been made more difficult by the rental trailer he had hauled behind him. He sat in the car holding his glasses in his left hand and rubbed his eyes with his right. He replaced his glasses and focused on the house and its surroundings. Til's car was parked there beside a strange Cadillac, and yet there was not a sound from within and no one in sight.

Phillip slipped from beneath the wheel of the car and walked to the kitchen door. He entered the empty kitchen and peered into the darkened parlor. He reached his hand inside to the parlor wall and switched on the light. A loud cheer erupted from the parlor. "Welcome home, Phillip!"

Huddled against the back wall of the parlor were Amanda, Til, Linda Vanstadt, Sherman Cooper, and brother Bill. They all began to talk at once. "Surprise!"

"Welcome home."

"How yah been?"

"Was the trip good?"

"Hi there."

"I'm Linda Vanstadt, Bill's friend."

Phillip smiled broadly and shook hands all around. He hugged Til and Amanda and accepted a can of cold beer from his brother. Suddenly he did a doubletake. Bill Zephries was dressed in purple—purple shirt and pants of some loose-fitting design, purple-toned shoes, and a gold chain around his neck. Phillip Zephries removed his glasses and blinked his eyes. "What the hell happened? You gone gay?"

Bill smiled and did a little dance and a turnaround. "No, man, this is what's happening. I'm a red-blooded horny toad and a rich American tourist."

The gathering laughed. Phillip stood with his arm around Amanda. "Do I have time for a shower before this party starts? I'm dusty from the trail."

Til said, "You better be hungry."

Phillip said, "I am. I am."

Bill stood holding hands with Linda Vanstadt. "You meet my girlfriend?"

"Yes, we met. Hello again."

The catch-up conversation continued for a few minutes.

Til moved beside Phillip and spoke in a low voice. "Sally Weeds called and say she want you to call her when you get time. Says it's important."

Amanda took Phillip's hand. "Bill, get Phillip's things from the car. Come on, Phillip, I want to show you to your room. We've done some things to it I think you'll like."

Amanda and Phillip went up the stairs. Sherman Cooper said, "Well, this is an occasion I think I'll have a drink." He went to the small bar in the corner of the room.

Til went to the kitchen, and Bill went to retrieve the bags.

Linda Vanstadt said, "I'll have one too, Mister Cooper. Gin and tonic, if you please."

"Bill's got this old bar stocked pretty good these days. Used to be bourbon and beer. Now it's everything from Perrier water to blush wines."

The young lady smiled in appreciation. "I stocked the bar, Mister Cooper."

The old man turned, surprised. "Oh, well, you have good taste. Very nice, very nice."

The two stood sipping their drinks. Sherman Cooper said, "What do you think of him?"

"Who?"

"Phillip."

"Oh, I don't like to make snap judgments, but he seems more studious than Bill."

"He graduated from MTSU."

"I heard that."

"Media."

"Yes, well, I never cared about those vocational schools."

"That's a rather unkind remark. MTSU is a fine university."

"That was a joke."

Upstairs, Phillip was saying, "This is nice, Amanda, but I don't see why you'd spend the money decorating when the place is up for sale. Or sold, for all it matters."

Amanda smoothed the pillows on the bed. "Sherman says we get thirty days' notice even after the deal is closed, and that's two weeks away." She turned and looked out the window at the wide expanse of the farm. "I wonder what they'll do with this house. It could be restored, you know . . . to its old beauty and charm. They do that in Williamson County. They have an Historical Society that preserves and protects old houses. I am told that there are not many houses still around like this one."

Phillip sat on the bed. "Why didn't we keep the house and just sell the farm?"

"We thought about it. I told Bill we could do that, and he said it wouldn't make sense to have an old house like this sitting in the middle of an industrial park or whatever they plan to do, and Sherman sniffed at the idea." Amanda sighed, "I sure hate to see it go."

Phillip stood and hugged his grandmother. "Look at the bright side. We can build another house just like this one somewhere if we want to."

"You think so? Could we? And you and Bill could have your own rooms, and privacy, and maybe a little office to do your advertising business in?"

Phillip smiled. "Now, Amanda, we are grown boys. It's not likely that we'd all live together. You don't want us underfoot all the time."

"I never minded having you underfoot before."

"Well, let's see how it works out."

On Beechcroft road, in the house trailer where she lived, Sally Weeds was rolling her blonde hair when the phone rang. She had to throw aside several pieces of clothing before she uncovered the phone in the clutter. "Hello."

"Sally?"

"Yes . . ."

"Phillip Zephries. You wanted me to call?"

Sally looked around the trailer as if being watched. "Yes, Phillip, I need to talk to you, but not on the phone."

There was a moment of silence. "Sally, if this is about Bill, I don't really want to get into it. I don't want to be involved."

"Well, no, it's not about Bill . . . er, that is, it, yes, it's about Bill; but it's about . . . you know, what we talked about before."

Phillip's voice became anxious. "Did you find out something?"

"I think so. Can we meet somewhere?"

"Not now, I just got here. They're fixing my dinner and all that. Are you working tomorrow?"

"I'll look and see. I'm just walking around farms showing people boundary lines and stuff. Let me see who's looking at what tomorrow." After a moment she said, "No, I don't have to go out in the morning."

"Are you in the real estate business too?"

"Naw, I just walk 'em around. If they get really interested another person goes with 'em. A lot of 'em are just tourists, and the salesmen get tired of hiking all day. It's hard to tell who's serious."

"I see. Well, I'll pick you up there at ten in the morning. How's that?"

"Okay, ten o'clock. How's Bill?"

"Looks all right to me. I'll see you in the morning."

Sally sat and stared at the phone for a minute. She pushed aside a half-eaten bowl of cold cereal and lit a cigarette. She looked around the cluttered trailer and kicked an old shoe box out of the way. Something new deep within made her aware of how much she cared for Phillip Zephries. He never talked dirty in front of her. He listened when she talked. In fact, he was the first man who had ever really listened when she talked. Why did Gorman and Bill always have to ask her to repeat everything she said? They didn't listen. They didn't care. They considered her some kind of bimbo.

Sally shook her head to ward off the feeling of anger and frustration. If she thought about it hard enough, she would start crying again. She had cried a lot lately, and she had done it while banging her fist against her pillow. She had married Gorman because she had been charmed by his attention. When she discovered his violent temper, things had gone too far. She married a man who beat her, cursed her, and threw fits of jealous rage. She could never decide about her emotions regarding the jealousy. She was flattered in a way. Her husband loved her so much he would get angry just thinking of someone else admiring his wife. And yet the rage was so frightening, so brutal, so crazy.

She had been running from Gorman for over two years now. She had gotten her divorce through the battered-wife people in Nashville, but even a court order could not keep Gorman from bursting into a place where she was working and causing a scene. He had been arrested and let go so many times she quit calling the authorities when she realized how slow and careful the law had to be.

That's why she had stayed close to Bill Zephries for so long. Gorman was afraid of Bill. Neither of them had any real respect for her, but Bill was not violent and could be a sweet and gentle person when he wanted to.

Now, she could feel Bill drifting away, taking her protection and her social life with him. She knew it wasn't love. She knew that. But how many women really stayed with a man for so simple a thing as love? She laughed at her own philosophy. And then she lay back on the small, cluttered sofa and started to cry.

Morning at the Old Zephries Place dawned brilliantly. Sunshine streamed through the bedroom window of Phillip Zephries. He luxuriated in the sun-dried sheets on his bed. The room smelled fresh. The new paint had taken away the musty smell that he had always associated with the old house. He was half awake when he heard a tapping on the door. He said, "Hello."

Linda Vanstadt peeped through the door and said, "Mornin'."

Phillip sat up quickly and pulled the covers over his bare chest. "Mornin'."

"Til sent up some coffee if you'd like it." The young woman wore a loose flowing, pastel-colored robe. Her sun-tanned legs were visible as she strode into the room and toward Phillip's bed. She set the tray on a bedside table. "I helped decorate this room. You like it?"

Phillip glanced about the room. "Oh, yes. Very nice."

"Bill was out early this morning. Went to Nashville on some business. Til's fixing what she refers to as your favorite breakfast. I thought I might have breakfast with you."

"Good. Good."

"Where did you learn to eat black-eyed peas, onions, and scrambled eggs together?"

Phillip felt at ease with the woman. He smiled. "I'm a bachelor. Breakfast is not a social affair with me."

"Well put. May I tell Til she can expect you downstairs shortly?"

"Yes, I'll be on down."

"Good morning." Linda Vanstadt left the room.

Phillip pulled back the white curtain, stared out the bedroom window for a moment, and muttered to himself, "I've got to find an apartment."

Linda Vanstadt walked into the kitchen where Til was cooking breakfast. Til looked up and said, "Ain't you dressed yet?"

"Phillip said he'd be down in a minute."

"Who said dat?"

"Phillip did. I took him some coffee."

"You took coffee to Phillip?"

"Yes."

"In dat outfit? Girl, is you crazy or somethin'? You can't go runnin' 'round here like no Barbie Doll takin' boys coffee. Dat's my job."

"He said he'd be right down. I'm going to get dressed."

"And put some shoes on. Don't folks in Nashville got no shoes? You gonna start somethin' 'round here you ain't careful. We got ways a doin' stuff and we stick to it mostly."

"You're just a jealous old nigger and you know it."

Til shook a spatula at the girl. "And don't be callin' me names. Folks hear you and think you're serious. "

"I am serious, you black witch."

Til whirled and playfully slapped the young woman on the back side with the spatula. "Get yo'self up them stairs and get some clothes on 'fore I go cut me a switch." As Linda Vanstadt left the room, Til was muttering, "Lawd, Lawd."

Phillip started down the hallway to the stairs and passed his brother's room. The door was open so he walked into the room and flipped on the light switch. His own room had been redecorated, but Bill's room was much the way it had been for years. Old faded high school banners hung from the walls. A scarred football lay on a table. Phillip picked it up and swung it back and forth with his passing arm. He held the ball in his right hand and stared at it. For the first time, he felt old. Pictures of the two brothers together were thumbtacked to the wall. Phillip looked at one of the old photographs and then caught sight of himself in the dressing mirror. He rubbed his hands through his thick hair and lifted his eyes to the ceiling. It was then that he detected the faint smell of marijuana. He wondered if Til or Amanda had noticed the smell and then realized that they probably wouldn't recognize it. He glanced toward the door and shook off the feeling that he was snooping.

He opened the door to the closet and slid the clothes on the hangers back and forth. In the back of the closet he found some faded jeans and an old Spring Hill Raiders football shirt. Phillip had long ago given such clothes to the Salvation Army in St. Louis. He took the clothes back to his room and tried them on. The fit was comfortable and the clothes smelled of soap and sunshine. He sat on the bed and tied the laces of an old pair of running shoes. He stood in front of the mirror and said to himself, "Welcome home, Phillip Zephries."

When Phillip drove to the curbside in front of Sally Weeds's trailer, he saw her walking down the street toward him. He stepped from the car and said, "Good morning."

Sally Weeds carried a brown paper bag in her arms. "I thought you was Bill there for a minute."

"These are his clothes."

"Was his clothes," Sally sniffed.

Phillip looked up and down the block. "I thought you had a car." Sally pointed to the Cheverolet Camaro parked in front of the trailer. "That's it there, but I couldn't get it started this morning. I felt like walking anyway. Reckon you can get it started?"

"What's it do?"

"Nothing. Starter, I reckon."

Phillip went to the car and raised the hood. He stood looking down into the mechanisms and complicated wiring for a minute. "Got a pair of pliers?"

"I don't have any tools."

He picked up a rock from the side of the street and banged away at the battery cables, knocking some of the corrosion from them. "Get in and try it now."

Sally fished in her purse for the keys, slid under the wheel, and started the car with ease. She shouted over the sound of the motor, "What'd you do?"

Phillip seemed pleased as he lowered the hood and slapped his hands together to knock the dirt from them. "Battery cables were loose. Better have them fix it next time you get gas."

"Thanks a lot." Sally shut the engine down and the two entered the cluttered trailer. Phillip pushed some clothes to one side of the sofa and sat down. Sally started removing things from the brown paper bag and putting them away. Phillip suddenly felt out of place in the trailer and in his clothes. He tried to sound light and casual. "That's a nice car."

Sally spoke without looking at him. "I paid for it."

Phillip coughed and muttered, "Yes, well . . ."

"Bill bought it for me, but I paid for it. Know what I mean?"

"Sure."

Sally sat down in a chair at the small dining table in the corner of the trailer. "I paid for it. The way girls like me get everything we get."

Phillip wanted desperately to change the subject. "Well, let's have it."

Sally lit a cigarette. "I met Gorman's mama at the store. He never took her to the hospital in Nashville. He was just going around town saying that to get himself an alibi for what he was really doin', which was shootin' at me and that nigger."

Phillip stared at the floor. He thought of his quiet, peaceful old apartment in St. Louis, his friends, his job. He looked wide-eyed at Sally. "Did you tell the police?"

"You and that nigger both said to shut up. No, I haven't told anybody but Gorman."

"You told Gorman?"

"I told him I'd tell the police if he ever bothered me again as long as he lived."

"What'd he say?"

"He started begging me to be quiet and started lying about it."

Phillip went to the door of the trailer. He spoke with his back to Sally. "What are we going to do about it?"

"I'm not doin' nothin 'bout it. I got him where I want him now. If he ever bothers me again, I'm puttin' the law on him. I told him so."

"Have you seen him lately?"

"No. Him and them Brannigan boys are working some-where over 'round Nashville on a construction project. I keep hopin' a truck'll run over him. You gonna tell that nigger?"

Phillip threw up his hands. "I don't know what to do."

"Well, you know how it is. Things regulate themselves."

Phillip Zephries stared at the blonde woman for a moment. "Thank you, Sally. Thanks for the good advice."

She shrugged her shoulders. "Phil, you've softened up a lot since you've been gone. You used to be tough when you played football. What happened?"

Phillip Zephries, who had felt superior to this country girl, hung his head and cleared his throat. "I don't know, Sally. I guess I've become too civilized, or thought I was civilized. Boy, the guy who said you can't go home again sure didn't know what he was talking about. It's the easiest damned place in the world to get to. I've been in this town for twenty-four hours, been in these clothes for thirty minutes, and suddenly I realize I've never been gone."

Sally snapped the top off a can of beer and handed it to him. "Well, let's have a beer and celebrate the return of that Sunday school son who came home that time."

"The prodigal son."

"Yeah, him."

Three beers later, and after much conversation about the old days of football and cheerleading, Sally Weeds closed the curtain that covered the only window in the small trailer, stepped behind a small curtain, and announced that she was going to change clothes and go into Nashville to ask about a new job. Phillip lay on the couch and stared at the curtain behind which Sally had disappeared. He finished the beer, walked toward the curtain, and slid it back on the thin rod that held it in place. Sally Weeds looked up from pulling a pair of jeans up over her knees. She straightened up and stood with her bare breasts pointed at the wide-eyed Phillip Zephries.

She buttoned her jeans and stared at the young man with a wry smile on her lips. She noticed the bulge in his jeans as she pulled a T-shirt over her breasts. She reached down and flipped his bulging groin with her finger, then kissed him on the cheek and said, "Phil, I liked your brother. I really did. I know that's over. I told him it was. I know what the car is for. I know good-bye when I hear and see it."

Phillip Zephries looked down at the floor and laughed. "Yeah, I know what the car was for."

Sally Weeds lit another cigarette. "You're not used to drinking beer at eleven in the morning, are you?"

"I guess not."

Phillip lay back on the sofa. "I've seen two partially naked women this morning. I guess it got to me."

"Oh, really? And who else?"

Phillip realized he could not say. "Oh, I was just reading one of those dirty magazines."

Sally sat in the small chair and looked amused at the bulge that was still in Phillip Zephries's pants. She stood and began to pull the T-shirt back over her head. "Take off your clothes, Phil."

"Hey, I'll be okay when I get some fresh air."

"Take off your clothes." Sally was naked and sat down on the sofa. She pushed Phillip back, placed her hand on his crotch, and kissed him on the mouth with a long, wet kiss.

Phillip Zephries groaned and said to no one in particular, "God, what a turkey I am."

Sally helped him off with his jeans. "You're not a turkey, you're a mockingbird."

Twenty minutes later, Phillip Zephries lay on the sofa and Sally Weeds returned from the small bathroom with a towel around her torso. The young man asked, "I'm a mockingbird? What did you mean by that?"

Sally Weeds laughed. "Did you ever see that mockingbird movie that Gregory Peck played in? I saw it the other night on the late show. They don't shoot mockingbirds." She laughed.

Suddenly Phillip felt threatened by the power of this seemingly harmless woman. He stood, pulled on his jeans, and took another beer from the refrigerator. "No, you're wrong, Sally. In Spring Hill, Tennessee, it's the bluebirds they don't shoot."

CHAPTER SEVEN

SIGN HERE, BOYS

Although the weather had been unseasonably warm during first part of April, the day of the closing of the sale of the Old Zephries Place dawned cloudy and cold.

Amanda came down the stairs dressed in a brown tweed business suit that had been brought out of mothballs for the occasion. She walked into the kitchen where Til was putting away the breakfast dishes, held herself erect, and said, "Til, it's like going to my own funeral."

Til wiped her hands on a paper towel and smiled at her mistress. "Why, Lawd, you look like a picture of health. You oughta dress up mo' often. It make you look ten years younger every time."

Amanda brushed the front of the tweed jacket with her hand. "You know something? I think I'd like to be buried in this outfit."

Til stepped behind her and straightened the collar of the jacket and squared the shoulders. "My, my, ain't we talking po' mouf today. We ain't gonna bury you in nothin'. You gonna outlive the whole mess of us. You want some coffee?"

Amanda sat down. "Yes, a half-cup. I've had plenty already."

Til set the coffee in front of the weary looking woman and went back to drying dishes, humming an old church song as she worked. Amanda sipped the coffee and picked a piece of lint from her jacket. "What time did they say they were picking me up?"

"I think dey said ten-thirty. You either gonna have dinner first and den sign, or sign and den have dinner. I don't 'member which come first. But I'm right sho' dey say ten-thirty. Are you up fo' it, you think?"

Just then they heard the front door open and close. Phillip came through the front room to the kitchen. He stopped at the door and spoke. "Good morning, ladies."

Amanda and Til mumbled a good morning. Phillip said, "I think winter's back. It's cold out there."

Amanda asked, "Bill's picking us up at ten-thirty?"

"Yes, it's almost time. He and Linda should be here any minute."

Amanda frowned. "Oh, is she going along? This is a family affair."

Phillip leaned against the door frame. "I thought so too. But you know Bill. He just said he and Linda would pick us up at ten-thirty. What can you do?"

Til said, "You get my medicine?"

Phillip straightened up. "Oh, yeah." He dug into his coat pockets. "Got it right here." He handed the black woman the small white bag. "I was beginning to wonder why I went to town."

There was the sound of a car in the parking area out back. The car door closed and Linda entered the kitchen with Bill holding the door open in front of her. When the two were in the room, there was an embarrassed silence. Linda wore a long raincoat over an expensive looking brown dress. She wore a slouch hat to the right side of her head and carried a small umbrella and matching purse. Bill wore a brown, pin-striped suit with an expensive silk tie over a pale blue shirt. Til was the first to comment. "My goodness! Y'all fixin' on gettin' married to boot?"

"Hey, ain't no sense gettin' a cow if you can get milk and butter without it," said Bill.

Linda Vanstadt elbowed him in the ribs. "I told you to be civil."

Bill feigned injury. "Oh, okay. We're going to the City Club for lunch after the deal is closed. Sherman's taking us."

Amanda ignored the high spirits of the two young people and excused herself. "I'll be right down if you're ready to leave now." She walked slowly toward the stairs to her room.

When Amanda had gone, Phillip said, "She's not having much fun with this. Maybe we should seem a little less jovial about it."

"Yeah, guess I got a little excited," said Bill, lighting a cigarette. "I never sold three million dollars' worth of real estate before. You think the deal's a straight one?" He motioned to Phillip.

Phillip cleaned his glasses with his handkerchief. "It's as near perfect as I can see it. I asked every question I could think of. But if something goes wrong, I don't want to be the architect of the deal. You know as much as I do."

Bill smiled and slapped his brother on the back. "Hey, lighten up, partner. I'm not gonna come down on you if something goes wrong. I just don't like the idea of long-term investments, that's all. You're the college kid around here. I trust you."

"I just told you not to trust me. You should have made some long-term investments. They're still negotiable, you know."

Til and Linda Vanstadt were in the corner of the room whispering. Til turned and spoke in a firm voice. "You boys hush up now. You gonna upset yo' grandmama and she ain't feeling too good anyway. Now, just hush."

Phillip lowered his voice and said to Bill, "I know you're handling your part of the deal your way, but I think one hundred thousand dollars in cash is a lot of money to be lying around."

Bill held his finger to his lips and whispered, "It's not going to be lying around. It takes money to make money. Don't worry about it. Okay?"

Phillip said, "It's your nickel."

Amanda seemed puzzled at the brevity of the transaction. There were two men representing the Japanese, Sherman Cooper representing the Zephries, and one secretary operating a copying machine.

Some of the copies had to be initialed, and Bill Zephries asked his brother in a whisper if he should print or write his initials.

Amanda sat with her arms folded and frowned at the shuffling of papers, the murmur of the secretarial work, and the dispassionate attitude of all involved.

Linda Vanstadt had not excused herself from the proceedings and sat holding each folder that was handed to Bill and then quickly passed on to her.

It was over in twenty minutes or less. Sherman Cooper shook hands with Phillip and Bill Zephries, hugged and kissed Amanda, and announced that they were ready for lunch. Amanda said, "Where were the Japanese? I thought we sold the place to the Japanese?"

Sherman Cooper held her hand. "Well, they have lawyers too. Everything's fine, just the way you wanted it."

Amanda sighed, "I'm just an old fogey. I guess I was expecting a band, or speeches or something." She held her head as if she were about to faint. "God rest the soul of Gyp Zephries," she said.

Sherman Cooper looked at her quizzically. He started the group through the office to the elevator. "We can walk from here to the Club. Do you feel like walking, Amanda?"

"Oh, yes, yes, I can walk. The air might do me good."

Linda Vanstadt had brought a new, expensive leather briefcase into which she was putting Bill's manila folders. She said to no one in particular, "I'm hungry."

Phillip and Bill Zephries were silent. They looked one another in the eye. The farm had been a bond that was now broken.

Bill said, "I'm thirsty!"

It was a tense lunch. Amanda nibbled at her food and kept bringing conversation back to the old days on the farm. Several prominent Nashvillians stopped by the table to speak to Sherman Cooper. Linda raved about the food. Bill drank an imported beer. Phillip sorted through his manila folders as if putting them in some kind of order, and Amanda kept reminding Bill that he should start the tractor and grade the driveway.

Over Bill's protest, Sherman Cooper insisted on buying lunch. He also suggested that Amanda be taken home, as she had had a long and trying day.

Amanda squeezed his hand and said, "Yes, I'd like one of Til's juleps and to get my feet up."

Bill said, "They can fix you a julep here."

Amanda scoffed, "No, no, I want one of Til's. The air's too heavy in here."

As Bill drove the Cadillac out of Nashville's downtown traffic and onto Interstate 65 South, the sun had broken through the clouds and blue skies were visible in the direction of Spring Hill. Linda Vanstadt rode in the front of the car with Bill. Phillip and Amanda were in the back. Linda had laid her hat on the seat and tossed her head to loosen her hair. The sun glistened on her brown locks as she turned in the front seat, placed her knees under her, and smiled at the occupants in the back. She tapped Bill on the shoulder and said, "Bill, don't you have something you want to say to your family?"

Bill Zephries cleared his throat and said, "Ahhh, Linda, I don't think . . ."

Linda interrupted, "Now, Bill, a deal's a deal. Let's have it."

Bill said, "Okay, you tell 'em."

Linda held her left hand up to display a large diamond ring. It sparkled in the sunlight streaming through the windows. She giggled, "Bill and I are going to be married."

Amanda and Phillip looked at one another. Phillip said, "Well, I, er, congratulations, best wishes . . . uh, all that." Amanda said, staring at the large diamond, "My Lord, how much did that cost?"

Bill frowned. "Amanda, you're not supposed to ask."

Linda said, "Amanda, I thought you'd be happy. We're going to have babies, your great-grandbabies."

"Oh, well, it suits me all right. I've just had too much news for one day. And besides that, young lady, I've raised enough babies in my time. When is this going to happen? Where?"

Linda bounced in the front seat and kissed Bill on the cheek. "We're going to get married in Las Vegas."

Both people in the back seat said, "Las Vegas?"

Linda pushed herself up higher in the front seat and patted her stomach. "We need to get married right away to stop wagging tongues, but this is just for the family's information," she laughed.

"My God, Linda," Bill said, "don't you have a secret in the world?" Linda kissed him on the cheek again.

"No, Daddy, not from my family. I don't want to start our marriage based on lies and secrets. And by the way, Amanda, the ring cost sixteen thousand dollars, tax included, of course."

Amanda seemed resigned. "Oh, I guess Bill can afford it. But mark my words — this money won't last forever."

Linda said, "Bill is going to build the greatest tobacco warehouse in the world. He's going to be Mister Tobacco. My granddaddy is helping him get a corporation together. Granddaddy can't get around much, but his mind is just as sharp as ever. I think they're right. Spring Hill needs its own warehouse."

Linda went on and on about the plans of her husband-to-be and the optimism she had about the future.

Once back at the Old Zephries Place, the group seemed wilted. Amanda said, "Til, come upstairs with me and help me off with this garb."

Bill loosened his tie, sat down at the kitchen table, and put his feet up on an extra chair. Til said, "Boy, you goin' to sleep why don't you get to bed?"

Phillip went upstairs to change, and Linda went to the bathroom. Bill helped himself to a beer from the refrigerator and murmured, "Cranky bunch of assholes."

Phillip came downstairs dressed in jeans and a sweatshirt. Bill recognized the old clothes as his and said, "Hey, man, don't you have any clothes of your own?"

Phillip pulled the tail of the sweatshirt down. "As a matter of fact, I don't. But this is not something you'll need in Las Vegas."

Bill sipped the beer. "How do you think it went over?"

"What?"

"Me and Linda?"

Phillip took a chair. "Oh, I think there were enough signals out to ease the blow."

"What do you mean?"

"You two have been acting married for a month or two."

"Really?"

"Yeah, really."

Bill lowered his feet to the floor and put his shoes on. "I guess you're right about that."

"When do you leave for Vegas?"

Linda came out of the rest room and sat down in Bill's lap. "What are you two tycoons talking about?"

Phillip said, "I wondered when you two are going west."

Linda kissed Bill on the cheek. "Tomorrow afternoon at 4:21, American Airlines to Dallas and then to Vegas. You want to go?"

Phillip said, "Who?"

Linda said, "You!"

Phillip took off his glasses and rubbed his eyes. "No, no, no, I'm no good at that. Besides," he laughed, "I don't have a thing to wear."

Linda laughed. "Oh, that reminds me. Bill, I've got some shopping to do and some packing. You'd better get me back to the apartment."

Til came stomping down the stairs. She entered the kitchen and scowled at the trio there. "Y'all 'bout wore that old lady out draggin' her 'roun town." She pointed at Linda Vanstadt. "Young lady, get off dat man's lap and come in here in de parlor and explain yo'self. I been hearing bad things 'bout you." She turned and went back into the front room.

Linda stood and smiled at the two men. "I'm in trouble with that old nigger now. I've stolen one of her children away." Linda shouted through the kitchen door to Til, "Hey, old nigger woman, you know anything 'bout birthin' babies?"

The young mother-to-be followed Til into the living room of the old house. The black woman had taken a seat on the edge of the sofa and sat leaning forward in anticipation of the story she hoped to hear. Linda said, "Now, I don't have time to talk to you all day. I've got things to do."

Til looked appraisingly at the young woman. "You sho' don't look big enough to have no baby if you ask me."

"I'm not going to have a baby."

Til exclaimed, "You ain't? Well, I heard you was having a baby with my own ears. What you tryin' to tell me?"

"I'm having twins."

Til frowned. "How you know dat? You don't know you gonna have no twins or no."

"I had an ultrasound yesterday, and the doctor says it's definitely twins."

Til stood and put her hands on her hips. "Now don't dat beat it all. Dey can tell dat way now?"

Linda said, "I knew you'd be happy."

Til said in mock anger, "Happy? What makes you think I'se happy 'bout it? Don't be bringing them babies 'round me. Lawd knows I ain't got no time for no babies. I already raised two of 'em. Dat's about all I want o' raising babies. And you gonna have to quit runnin' 'round barefooted all de time now. Worms get out of the dirt and get up through yo' feet and it makes de babies have worms."

"Where on earth did you hear a thing like that?"

"See? I knowed you don't know nothin' 'bout having babies. Everybody knows dat."

Linda came toward Til and hugged her tightly. "You're going to be a very valuable help to these kids. I can see that right now."

Til started to cry. She jerked away from Linda and wiped away a tear. "Young lady, you gonna have to clean up yo' mouf and straighten yo'self up now. I'se gonna need all the help I can get if we gonna have new babies 'round here."

CHAPTER EIGHT

HOMECOMING

The ambulance came at two in the morning. Til had been in her bedroom when she heard a thumping noise and rushed to the bottom of the stairwell to find Amanda Zephries slumped on the floor, victim of a stroke that paralyzed her left side.

It had happened four days after the sale of the old homeplace. Phil had been awakened by Til's screams. He had called the ambulance that took Amanda to the hospital in Nashville where the stroke had been diagnosed.

Mister and Missus Bill and Linda Zephries were recalled from Las Vegas where they had just been married. Til had set up housekeeping in one of the rooms of the suite where Amanda lay ill. Phillip sat by the bedside of his grandmother. "Amanda? Do you know me? It's Phillip." He wiped her brow with a cold cloth. "Can you hear me? The nurse says you can use this board to answer yes or no. Amanda?"

The left side of Amanda Zephries's face was drooped and lifeless. She occasionally touched it unbelievingly with her right hand. She stared straight ahead. Phillip held the board before her eyes, "Amanda? Point to yes if you know me."

Amanda turned her head slightly, without expression, toward the young man. She pointed a shaky finger at the word "yes" painted in blue letters on the board.

Phillip jumped. He turned to no one in the room and said, "She knows me." He stood and ran to the next room where Til was sleeping on a sofa and shook her awake. "Til, she knows me. She pointed to yes on the board. She knows me."

Til jumped to her feet and went to Amanda's bedside. "I knowed you was gonna be all right. I prayed 'bout it. I just knowed it." She held the old woman's paralyzed left hand. She grabbed the board and held it to Amanda's eyes. "Point to yes and tell you know me. Just point where it say yes, right there. Point." Amanda Zephries looked blankly at Til. She raised her right hand and knocked the small board to the floor. The old woman then started coughing, shaking, and gasping for breath. Til broke into tears. "Get de doctor quick! She havin' one of dem spells. Get 'em quick."

A nurse came into the room. She began to raise the bed and reach for an oxygen mask at the same time. She soon quieted Amanda and ushered Phillip and Til from the room. The nurse called Phillip out into the hall. She spoke calmly. "I don't think it's a good idea to have that woman here all the time. She's hysterical. It's not good for the patient."

Phillip wiped his brow and spoke in a shaky voice. "It's my fault. I woke her up. My grandmother recognized me. She pointed to yes on the board. I'm sorry I got carried away."

The nurse made a note on her chart. "That's good news. Your grandmother is in shock. That's good news that she recognized you. Don't try to press her into long conversations. Smile as much as possible; reassure her all you can. But that black woman must try to calm herself. You'll have to talk to her."

Phillip hung his head. "I will. But she won't leave. They've been together for almost thirty years."

The nurse looked toward the suite of rooms in awe. "Thirty years?"

Amanda Zephries lay in the hospital bed and watched as Til seemed to go mad. Amanda spoke with her eyes. "What in the world is the matter with that old nigger, damn her soul, holding up a board to see if I know the difference between yes and no? What's she doing here anyway? Why isn't she back with my babies? They are by that stove and she's here and the fire will go out and they'll freeze. God, I'm so alone in here. Can't they see me? What's wrong with them? Why can't they understand that I want to go home to my babies? I can't make them hear me. Gyp, please get me out of here. Let's go to Nashville and have dinner. We'll take the Packard and you can drive if you promise not to drink too much. Let's get away from all of this. Please, Gyp, can't you see how I need you?"

Bill and Linda Zephries came straight to the hospital from the airport. They looked weary from the sudden departure and the long flight. Bill seemed half drunk and half hung over. Linda had managed to freshen up on the plane.

Phillip explained all he knew about the event. He told them that Amanda had not fallen down the stairs but had fallen at the bottom step and had not seriously hurt herself in the fall. He explained that Amanda was sleeping. Linda and Bill stood in the doorway of her room and looked at the sleeping woman. Bill said, "My God, look at her face."

Amanda Zephries's facial muscles had given way on the left side and drooped grotesquely.

Phillip urged them back into the sitting room of the suite. "She's not in pain. The doctor says she's just confused at the moment. He says therapy might bring her back to near normal. It's too early to tell though."

Bill looked around the room. "Where's Til?"

"I had Sally take her to get some things from the house."

"Sally?"

"Sally Weeds. I couldn't think of anyone else."

Bill shrugged. "It's okay."

Phillip sat down on the sofa. "The doctor put Til on valium, and she calmed down. I've been through hell here."

Bill put his arm around his brother. "Sorry, cowboy, I got here as soon as I could."

Phillip managed a smile. "I didn't mean that the way it sounded. I'm just feeling sorry for myself. Look, why don't you two get on home, get some sleep, and relieve me in the morning? There's not much you can do anyway."

Linda, who had been silent, said, "Poor darling, I hate to leave her here."

Phillip said, "No, you two go on. I'll be here in the morning. I've got everything I need and Til is coming back in an hour or so."

Bill turned to Linda. "Tell me what to do. I'm dingy as hell."

Linda took his hand. "Come on." She said to Phillip, "We'll be here early in the morning. Call if you need us before then. My apartment is not far from here on West End. You've got the number."

"Yes, I have it."

Bill walked to Amanda's door and whispered, "Good night, sweetheart." He turned to Phillip, "Has Sherman been here?"

"Oh, yes, he sat up all night. He was exhausted. I was worried about him. I sent him home."

Linda placed her hand at her mouth and coughed lightly. "Did he think the trauma of selling the farm had anything to do with it?"

Bill and Phillip looked at one another. It was not a question either one of them wanted to pose. Phillip said, "He thinks so."

Bill said, "Has she spoken at all since this happened?"

Phillip lowered his head. "She's only said one word since she's been here."

Bill said, "And?"

"Gyp," Phillip said.

Phillip was dozing on the sofa of the hospital suite when the phone rang. He picked it up and whispered, "Hello."

"Phil, this is Sally. I'm at your house."

"What is it?"

"Well, Til was real groggy when she got here. She said she wanted to put her feet up a minute, and now she's sound asleep. I don't know what to do."

Phillip sat up on the sofa and rubbed his eyes, "Well, don't wake her up. She hasn't slept in days."

"I'm at the kitchen phone."

"Well, talk low."

"What do you want me to do?"

"Why don't you go up to my room and get some sleep? When Til wakes up she'll find you. Get some sleep. My room is up the stairs and—"

"I know where your room is."

"Yeah, well . . . Go up there and lie down for a while."

"I'm hungry. I didn't eat anything all day, you know."

"Well, see what there is to eat there. There must be something."

"It's spooky out here."

"Just eat something and get some sleep. Call me if anything happens. Lock the doors. Is Til in her own bed?"

"Yeah, she's got all her clothes on, and her shoes, but she's in bed."

"Let her sleep, okay?"

"Okay. I'll call you if I need anything."

Sally peeked into the small bedroom off the kitchen. Til slept with one arm hanging off the side of her single bed. Sally tiptoed into the room and lifted the sleeping woman's arm back onto the bed and removed her shoes. Til stirred but didn't wake up. Sally stepped out of the room, leaving the door ajar. She opened the refrigerator and found meat for a sandwich. She worked quietly as she prepared a sandwich and poured a glass of milk. She sat at the kitchen table and listened for sounds other than those of Til's breathing. A dog barked somewhere outside and far away, the wind rustled the leaves of the trees, and a car went past the house without pause.

Sally went quietly upstairs. She turned at the top of the stairs and started toward Phillip's room. The door to Bill's room was open. She stepped inside and was overwhelmed with familiar smells. She listened for more sounds. There was none that was unfamiliar.

The blonde woman unbuttoned her blouse, took it off, and dropped it on the familiar bed. She reached into the closet and got a blue cowboy shirt. She slipped it over her bare breasts and buttoned it. She threw herself across the bed and slept.

Rosanna Zephries got off the elevator on the floor where Amanda lay ill.

Forty-eight years old, emotionally scarred and hardened, she had come back to Tennessee with revenge and vindication stirring in her blood. She carried a small black briefcase and wore a black pantsuit covered by a silky black floor-length coat. She seemed a witch-like creature as she made her way to Amanda Zephries's room. A nurse stopped her in the hallway and asked, "May I help you?"

"I'm Mrs. Zephries's daughter-in-law. I just got to town."

"She's there in that room. I'm afraid she's asleep though. I wouldn't awaken her. Would you like to speak to the nurse in charge?"

"I won't disturb her, thank you."

As Rosanna Zephries stepped into the dimly lit room, Amanda stirred in her bed. Rosanna, now a real estate executive of San Francisco, took the chair at the bedside of her former mother-in-law. She pulled the chair close to the bed and spoke in a firm voice. "Amanda. Can you hear me? Amanda, it's me, Rosanna, come back after all these years. Rosanna, remember?" The woman leaned even closer to the patient. "Don't you die on me, you old bitch. Don't you take this moment from me. Not after these years of torture, don't you deny me." Rosanna Zephries slapped the distorted face of the helpless Amanda. "Look at me! Speak to me!"

The dark figure huddled by the bedside sat silent for an eerie moment. She stood and went to the light switch by the door. She flipped on the bright overhead light and stared at the bedridden woman in defiance. She went back to the chair, fumbled with the latch on the briefcase, and retrieved a sheaf of papers. She held the papers to the old woman's face. "Look, Amanda. I own the Old Zephries Place. I own it. I got your house as my commission. I own your house, you daughter of Satan. Look at me! Say something, you bitch!"

A voice came from behind Rosanna Zephries. "That's enough. That's enough. Leave her alone."

Rosanna Zephries whirled in the chair and faced her son for the first time in twenty-seven years. "Phillip. Oh, God, Phillip."

Phillip grabbed his mother by the arm, and papers flew across the floor. He flipped off the light switch and pushed his mother into the other room. The woman backed into a chair and plopped down in it. She sat staring defiantly. Phillip stood breathless in the center of the room. He stared at his mother. She looked first to the right and then to the left, never at her son. The young man leaned toward her. He spoke softly, "Where have you been?"

The woman stared at the wall. There was a long silence. Phillip repeated the question, almost as if he were speaking to himself. "Where have you been all this time?"

Rosanna Zephries chewed on her lower lip. "My God, Phillip, what a question." She looked painfully at her son. "What a question."

Phillip backed toward the sofa and plopped down on it. He put his head in his hands. He started to laugh, then raised his head and saw his mother staring at him. He began to laugh again. He stopped suddenly, stood, and smiled at the dark woman crouched in the chair. "Hi, Mom. Gee, nice to see you. I met my brother George. Isn't he a handsome young man? I'm glad you stayed in touch with him."

Rosanna Zephries said bitterly, "He didn't have Amanda for a grandmother."

"Oh, sure," Phillip said. "Amanda's not feeling well, you know. How's it going? Heard you say you bought the old home place. That's nice. I hope it's a nice investment for you."

Rosanna frowned at her son. "I didn't buy the farm. I own the house and ten acres. That's all. A sort of finder's fee."

Phillip threw his hands in the air. "Oh, sorry about the little technicality. I'm new in real estate myself."

"I know that."

Rosanna Zephries got up from her chair, went quickly to the other room, and started gathering her papers from the floor. She snapped her briefcase closed and stood with it in front of her as if it were a shield. She spoke in a quiet, determined voice. "Phillip, I didn't come here in hopes of a reunion. I know you hate me. You should. You've had expert training in hating. A great teacher of hate and distrust and selfishness. I lost you as a son a million nights ago. I know that. I've faced it. I dealt with it."

The woman put her hand on the door. Phillip said, "Where are you going? You can't just — "

Rosanna Zephries interrupted. "Young man," she pointed to the bed of Amanda Zephries, "I hope I'm going to a funeral."

CHAPTER NINE

ASHES, ASHES, ASHES

Amanda Zephries passed away on the morning of May 13, 1986, as a result of complications of a stroke.

There were no written funeral plans in the will. Sherman Cooper said he had spoken of them to Amanda when she was alive, and so the service and the burial went as he instructed.

Sherman Cooper called together the family, except for Rosanna, a week after the funeral of Amanda Zephries. The old lawyer made his way through cardboard boxes and assorted junk on his way to the parlor of the old house. Til was kneeling searching through one of the boxes for something.

"Howdy, Til. Is everybody moving out at once?"

Til stood and stretched her back. "Naw, ain't nobody gone no place yet. We just draggin' stuff out and draggin' it back. Never knowed we had this much stuff in this house. Linda won't let us move dis old furniture. She puttin' tags on everything. Lawd knows what she want with dis old stuff."

"Where is everybody?"

"Phillip is upstairs. Bill and Linda 'sposed to be here in a minute. You want some coffee?"

"No thanks. I'll wait in the parlor. Did you find an apartment?"

"Lawd, no. Did you ever know what they want for one of dem little old cubby holes? I'se movin' in wid one of my friends 'til I can get de rent right."

Sherman Cooper shook his head in understanding. "Housing is expensive these days. Especially in Spring Hill. You might want to get out of the area and look around."

Til went back to her work muttering, "I sho' might, I sho' might oughta do dat."

Sherman Cooper sat in the parlor and stared at the walls. He settled back in the big leather chair in which he had sat for so many years. He crossed his legs and shook his shoulders back into the soft leather. The doors of the house were open, so he could hear the birds singing, squirrels scampering across the roof, and the general hum of nature's springtime. He removed his glasses, laid them in his lap, and fell asleep.

Linda Zephries was first to enter the room and find the old counselor in slumber. She put her finger to her lips and quieted Bill, who was right behind her. The two took seats on the sofa and intercepted Phillip as he came down the stairs. Linda said, "Shhhh," and pointed at Sherman Cooper who was breathing deeply as he slept. The three sat in amused silence for a minute before Linda said in a loud voice, "The court will now come to order." She stomped her foot on the floor.

Sherman bolted upright in the chair and began to search for his glasses. The trio laughed. The old man placed his glasses on his nose and joined the laughter as he caught sight of the three people seated on the sofa. "Sorry. I dozed off there for a minute. Spring fever, don't you suppose?"

Phillip said, "I just woke up myself. This weather will put lead in your britches."

Bill Zephries was in a grumpy mood. He crossed his legs and knocked an imaginary spot of dust from his shoe. "As soon as we're all awake, let's get on with this."

Sherman reached for his briefcase. "We'll need Til in here if somebody will holler at her."

Linda went to the door of the kitchen. "Til, will you come in here, please?"

Til came into the room wiping dirt from her hands with a soiled cloth. "I'se diggin' up my azalea bushes. Yo' mama ain't gettin' dem bushes just 'cause she own de rest of dis place."

Sherman Cooper cleared his throat and started shuffling through a stack of papers. He asked offhandedly, "Has she been out here?"

Bill said, "Hell, no. She knows I'd kick her ass. But she's still down there in her suite at Spence Manor."

Sherman said, "Well, that's the other thing. I think I've got you off that disturbance thing. She didn't press charges."

Bill sulked back on the sofa and murmured an obscenity. He resented Sherman mentioning the embarrassing incident. He had been doing some cocaine in the parking lot of the Hall of Fame Motor Inn when the outrage of his mother's return had hit him. He had suddenly realized that he was just a block or so from where she was staying at Spence Manor. He had walked the two blocks and had been denied entrance to the place. That's when he had lost his temper and, as Til had put it, "thrown a fit." Bill shook the guilty fog from his head and stared at his hands folded in his lap.

Sherman said, "Now, this is fairly simple about the will. Amanda gave you boys everything before she died, so there are just a few personal items and some things in her lockbox that she left to Til and some money for the church. I've notified the church, and I have Til's things here. I think someone should look after these investments for you, Til. I'd be happy to do it."

Til looked around the room. "I think I gonna let Linda look after it if she will."

Linda said, "I'll be glad to."

Sherman Cooper handed the folder to Linda Zephries. "It's all in there." He looked at Til, who was still standing.

Til said, "Tell us all what it is."

Sherman said, "Well, it's very generous really. Several thousand in savings bonds, some stock certificates, and personal items here in the house. You boys own what Linda tells me is some very valuable antique furniture in this house."

Bill said, "I was under the impression that Amanda had plenty of money."

Sherman said, "She had plenty of land. Not much money."

Phillip stood. "But how . . . I mean, what happened to it?"

Sherman Cooper also stood. "Boys, I'm not sure this is the proper thing to do, but I've thought about it and I guess you need to know. Phillip, the money to put you through college, the money to help operate this place . . . I don't know, look around you. The money came from Rosanna . . . your mother."

There was an electric silence in the room. Bill Zephries stood quickly as if he had just awakened. He pointed a finger at Sherman Cooper. "Are you telling me . . . uh, are you saying that . . . my, Rosanna Zephries, Atworth, whatever, has been supporting us and this place all these years?"

Sherman Cooper opened his hands palms up. "She got everything at the death of her second husband. She became a whiz in the real estate business with some of the money, and lately she's made a small fortune of her own. She's no nitwit."

Phillip looked Sherman Cooper in the eye. "Why? Why did she do it? Why didn't she contact us?"

"Well, this is personal, I know, but she did it because she loved her children."

Bill said, "Bullshit."

Til said, "Lawd, Lawd."

146

Sherman continued. "She married a black, and she didn't want to interrupt your lives with her troubles. When she learned that the farm was for sale, she took the idea to the Japanese firm that bought it. I think the idea got out of hand."

Phillip walked around the room. "Sherman, tell me, how do you know all this?"

"I've talked to her off and on for twenty years."

Linda could stay quiet no longer. She asked, "Do you mean you've known everything all along? You kept that secret from these boys that long? God, you surprise me."

Bill said, "You knew she was buying this house?"

Sherman held up his hands. "Now wait a minute, all of you. I knew nothing about her involvement in the sale of this property, nothing. That's why I say it got out of hand. She stayed in the background on this thing until the very end. I was as surprised as you were to find she was in town."

Phillip said, "Amanda knew everything all along."

Sherman said, "Everything."

Bill said, "She never told us anything."

Phillip moaned, "Why? Sherman, why didn't you say something?"

The old lawyer shook his head and stared at the floor. "There was never a time. This started when you were five or six years old. You weren't even in school when Rosanna contacted me to contact Amanda. There was just never a time."

Phillip said, "George Atworth is our brother?"

Sherman said flatly, "He's your half-brother."

Sherman Cooper picked up his briefcase, snapped it shut, looked around the room and said in a low voice, "I think you're a fine family with a good future if you'll put all this behind you and get on with your lives. But let me say this: Rosanna is not a bad person. She's had hard decisions to make and she made them. But she has always cared what happened and has made the best of a terrible situation. I'd like to go now, if there are no questions."

Phillip said, "No questions. Thank you, Sherman."

Widow Weeds was sweeping her front porch. The Widow was a talker, and in the absence of someone else to talk to she talked to herself. She was saying, "These trucks and cars that these Saturn people are driving around here are blowing all kinds of dust and stuff all over my porch and yard. Maybe I'll go down to one of them meetings and get up and tell 'em to put some money on the side to help us folks clean up after 'em. They got so many million dollars I don't see how they'd miss a little bit of clean-up money. I could paint the porch gray and get me a new swing out here and it'd make this place look a sight better if you ask me."

She swept faster with the plan formulating in her mind. "I could put me up some bluebird boxes out back and help out with housing the bluebirds. I don't think bluebirds are gonna want to live over there around that factory anyway. Mister Elbert feeds his birds all winter, and he says bluebirds don't even like people, let alone factories."

Widow Weeds heard a phone ringing. She jerked the broom to port arms and half ran to the screen door. There she dropped the broom and ran to the phone. She picked up the receiver and said sweetly but breathlessly, "Hello."

The voice on the other end of the line was that of her son, Gorman. "Mama?"

"Yes, honey."

"Gorman."

"I know. What is it?"

"What's goin' on over there?"

"I was just sweeping the porch. It gets all covered with dust and stuff from all this traffic since they's so much traffic, as you know. I was just thinking I might go to one of them meetings and tell 'em what I think of all this mess they making over here in this neighborhood."

"Yeah, I know, Mama. What's goin' on besides that?"

Widow Weeds knew that Gorman wanted to talk about Sally, but she thought she could steer the conversation away from her son's love life to the more important goings on in the little town. She placed her elbows on the table in her most talkative stance and said, "I don't think you heard about them closing Freeland Road, did you? They closed it down like bingo. Never said a word to a soul, and it being a public road everybody's upset about them taking over public places just 'cause the road run through there like it did. I mean the Saturn property. I was telling Thelma the other day, what they oughta do is — "

Gorman interrupted. "Mama, that was two months ago. I don't care anything 'bout Freeland Road. Bill Zephries got married, didn't he?"

Widow Weeds was silent for a moment. "Uh, yes, honey, he did. Married some girl from over there in Nashville. Did you ever know her?"

"Course I don't know her. Have you seen Sally?"

She took her elbows from the table and spoke haltingly. "No, I ain't seen her."

"You hear about her?"

"Course I hear about her. She was my daughter-in-law."

"Well?"

"Gorman, why don't you forget about Sally? Can't you meet some nice girls over there in Nashville?"

"What did you hear?"

Widow Weeds held the phone and stared at it for a second then said, "Bill's been back down there, and just a day or two before he was married."

"Go on with the rest of it then." Gorman sounded angry.

"Well, you know Thelma lives right across the street from her trailer. Sally's selling real estate now. Some of them real estate people come by now and then. You know Thelma lives right there and can't help seeing what goes on. It's as plain as the nose on your face. You know, I don't nose around in that 'cause I figure it ain't none of my business, and it sure ain't none of Thelma's—"

"Mama! Just tell me!"

"Well, the other afternoon, right when he was gettin' married, Bill come down there dressed in them old sloppy jeans and that school sweatshirt and spent the whole afternoon, and Thelma said there was a bunch of beer cans in the trash the next day, so I blame Sally for that because she says they all through with seein' each other and everything, and then there she goes and gets him in the trailer and him gettin' married, and it seems a shame right in broad daylight too."

Gorman was silent for a moment, then said quietly, "Mama, you know how you took up for Sally against me? Now what are you gonna say 'bout that? Maybe I was right all along, don't you reckon?"

"Now, Gorman, don't get to wrestling around with that and start no trouble. It's not our business what the Zephries do, or Sally either for that matter, and I'll be glad when they gone from here for good. They got to go someplace in two weeks 'cause they bein' thrown out of that house, and you heard about that, of course."

"I heard, Mama, I heard."

CHAPTER TEN

ALLIANCES

Sally Weeds's trailer was gutted by fire three days after Gorman Weeds decided that Bill Zephries was going to continue his relationship with the woman.

Sally was not at home at the time. Investigators said it was an accidental electrical fire.

A tearful, frightened Sally Weeds called Phillip Zephries at two A.M. to report on the fire and beg for a talk. Til Jefferson answered the phone expecting bad news and got it. "Til, this is Sally. Is Phillip there? My trailer is burned down."

Although Til had moved most of her belongings to her friend's house, she stayed on at the Old Zephries Place until Phillip had cleared out his personal things. Bill had taken an old football and his rifle and a few clothes.

Til yawned into the phone. "Girl, you don't call dis number when they's a fire, you call de fire department."

Sally sounded angry. "You just tell me is Phillip there, that's all."

"He here all right, but he be sleepin' like a person should dis time of night."

"Well, tell him I'm comin' up there right now. It's more important than you know." Sally slammed down the phone.

Sally and Phillip sat drinking coffee at the old kitchen table. Phillip was trying to calm her. "Sally, I know it was an electrical fire, I know Gorman does electrical work in construction, and I know he could have made the fire look like an accident, but I don't see how we can get involved. We're talking about attempted murder, arson, and hell knows what all, and we can't prove anything."

Sally dried her red eyes. "Where will he stop? How can I stop him?"

Phillip said, "Look, Sally, I know how you feel. There are a million divorced women in this country who are in the same situation. Let's be calm for a minute and try to think."

There was silence as the two sat watching dawn arrive over the old hills. Sally said, "I could kill him." She said it flatly and sincerely.

Phillip held up his hands palms out. "Whoa now. Don't even say that as a joke. That scares me. Things get started like that. No, no."

"I'm not jokin'. He needs killin'. Somebody should."

"Well, not either one of us."

Phillip walked to the kitchen window. He turned and said, "It's going to be a nice day."

Sally said, "Big deal."

"Hey, let's be realistic for a minute," Phillip said. "If we take this to the law, we got a bunch of people involved. There's Bill, George Atworth, you, me, and God knows who else they'd drag into it. And Muff and Puff would swear he was with them. They'd swear the sun didn't come up that day if he'd ask them. He keeps them in work. He brings them into these jobs with him. It's almost as if they worked for him." Phillip bit his lip, "And how come we didn't report the shooting until now? Explain that."

Sally started to cry again. Phillip said, "Oh, come on, don't do that."

Sally Weeds took Phillip's hands and held on. "Phillip, I'm worried. He knows you were there that afternoon."

Phillip's eyes widened. "Me? You think he's after me?"

"That's what I'm afraid of. It's a little ol' bitty town, Phillip. It's not like St. Louis. Everybody knows everything after a day or two."

Phillip held his hands out as if to embrace his surroundings. "What am I doing in this damned place? What keeps me here? It's as if I were six years old again. I'm playing in the woods, sleeping all afternoon, drinking beer all night, and eating like a starved field hand. What is it about this damned place anyway?"

Til came into the room. "Y'all want mo' coffee?"

"Morning. No, we've had enough coffee, I think."

Sally said, "None for me either."

Phillip said to Sally, "Where are you going to sleep? Have you had any sleep?"

"No."

Phillip motioned upstairs. "Well, you can sleep up there until you find a place. Soon though, we're leaving here, in a few days."

Sally looked down at her smudged clothes. "I need a few things."

"What kind of things?"

"Well, I don't know. I lost everything in the fire."

"Oh, yeah. Well, you got some money?"

"I get paid tomorrow."

"How much you need?"

"I don't know. I . . ."

"Here's a hundred dollars. Get some, uh, things."

Sally took the money and went to the door of the kitchen. She turned, "Thanks, Phillip. I appreciate everything. I'll be back after a while. Bye. Bye, Til."

Til said, "Uh huh."

Phillip sat back down in the chair by the kitchen table. Til turned at the kitchen sink and stared at him. "What you think you doin', boy?"

"What?"

"What you think you doin' is what I said. You gonna move dat woman in here and give her money to buy stuff and her old man lookin' to kill her and likely to kill you too. You crazy boy. Let dat woman go on."

Phillip threw his hands up. "Aw, Til, you can't just throw a person out on the street. Where's she gonna go, for Christ's sake?"

"It ain't none of yo' business where she go. Dat's what I say. Let dat woman go."

It was late that night when Phillip walked into the room where Sally Weeds had gone to bed. She lay with one long leg stretched from under the bedcovers. She had bought a shorty nightgown that day. A shaft of dim light came from a partially closed closet door. Phillip asked, "Are you asleep?"

Sally Weeds spoke in a soft, liquid voice, "No, honey, come on in."

Sherman Cooper sat across the room from Rosanna Zephries in her suite at Spence Manor. Rosanna stood by the window and looked out at the late May sunshine. "You told them everything?"

Sherman Cooper tamped tobacco into his pipe. "I can't see that it matters now."

Rosanna tightened the belt of her expensive dressing gown as she swept across the room. She picked up a glass of iced orange juice from a table and sat on a small, straight-backed chair. She pointed a finger at Sherman Cooper. "This dream, this plan, this madness of mine — what did you think of it? And forget for a minute that you're a lawyer."

Sherman smiled. "We don't forget we're lawyers until we become judges." He puffed his pipe. "I understand it, I guess. So many years. So much frustration. I'm frankly surprised you waited this late in the game. When you first left the Old Zephries Place, that became a hassle because you legally abandoned the children. When you discovered the boys were doing great in school, you didn't want to disrupt their lives with a lawsuit, and when they were finally grown you came up with this other plan. I don't know what else you could have done."

Rosanna pursed her lips and stared blankly at the wall. "It's been one damned trap after another." She wiped tears from her eyes. "You know, Sherman, I had this vision. Listen to this. I was going to walk onto the front porch of the Old Zephries Place and Amanda would be sitting there. I was going to arrive in a white limo, by the way. And I was going to step out in all my fashionable splendor and say, 'I am the new owner of this house. Get off my property immediately.'"

Sherman said, "I know."

"My God, I lived that scene. You know the sun was going to be shining. I was going to take my two sons into my arms and tell them of her wicked ways. I was going to follow them as they bounded to the limo to ride away with me." The sad-eyed woman wiped away tears. "They never grew up, you know? Not in my mind's eye. They were still little boys with bare feet and freckled faces. My God, my God, I gave my life to it, and it seems it drove me mad. Do you think I'm mad, Sherman?"

Sherman Cooper creased the leg of his trousers with his fingers and looked up at the troubled woman. "You certainly don't have a monopoly on it. Know what I've been thinking of doing?"

Rosanna seemed surprised at this confidence. "What?"

Sherman stood and hitched up his trousers. "Rosanna, I have been lying awake nights planning a trip."

"What kind of trip?"

"I have been thinking of buying a horse, full saddle gear, a gun, of course, and riding through the mountains. Sleeping by the trail, eating from a tin pan, coffee over an open fire, and playing the harmonica. I've been taking riding lessons."

Rosanna Zephries burst into laughter. "If you're trying to make me feel better, you've done it."

"No, no, wait. At night, after a few martinis, alone in that goddamned apartment with nothing I'm interested in reading but Louis L'Amour, I get serious about it. I think I'm really going to do it. I wonder why I don't?"

Rosanna sipped the orange juice. "What you're saying is that I've done it. I tried to play out the fantasy."

The lawyer snapped back from his trance-like thoughts. "I'm just sharing with you, that's all." He sat back down in the chair. "Just sharing."

Rosanna Zephries started to speak when the phone rang. "Hello. Yes. Who's calling, please?" She turned to Sherman with her hand over the mouthpiece. "It's Linda, Bill's wife."

Sherman Cooper shrugged. "Talk to her."

Rosanna Zephries held the phone for a decisive moment. She spoke into the receiver. "Hello. Yes." There was a pause. "Yes, I know." There was another pause. "I'll be leaving town the day after tomorrow. It would have to be tomorrow." There was another pause. "Very well. Good-bye."

Rosanna Zephries turned to Sherman Cooper. "She wants to talk."

"That's good. Very good."

Rosanna folded her arms across her breasts as if she were chilled and added, "About real estate."

CHAPTER ELEVEN

HOW MUCH AM I BID?

Sherman Cooper never smoked cigarettes in public. He smoked them privately because they seemed to bring back his youth. He also mixed his own vodka martinis in a crystal mixer and sipped them with a cup of hot tea. Sherman did not like the idea of getting old or dying. Life had been fun for him despite the tragedy of his wife. He had taken chances. He had approached his adventures at the right time and had not been trapped by any serious confrontations on any account. He pondered a line by the poet Miller Williams, something about when your hands start to look like your father's hands. The old man studied the hand that held the cigarette. He thought he could remember his father's hands being much older. He sipped the martini and followed it with a sip of the hot tea. Sherman Cooper was drunk. He sang a song, "Whistle to me sweet Lorraine, just before I catch the train, I will know that you're in love with me."

And he would buy the horse. A big red horse with a white mane, wide at the shoulder, and sharp of ear. The horse must listen closely for sounds that could invade the solitude of his ride through the wilderness. Sherman couldn't be bothered with the listening. He would be playing the harmonica as he rode through the beautiful trees. Yes! Oh, yes! There, in a draw, he would find a secret spring. He would drink from it and find himself young again, smooth of hand, and bursting with energy.

Sherman Cooper leaned back in his chair and allowed his mind to drift to the affairs of the Zephries family. He had confidence that they could iron out their problems. He had every intention of trying to help them, and his counselor's nature caused him to almost welcome the challenge. He was running their various problems through his mind and remembered that at lunch with old pals from the legal profession he had learned, and been warned, that Bill Zephries was using cocaine. Running with the wrong crowd while his wife was out shopping and decorating the new condo. Bill Zephries had tried the new, safe Cadillac of drugs, cocaine, and had found it much to his liking.

The old man was dozing, riding his big red horse through the Appalachians.

Linda Zephries took particular care in dressing. She was to meet her mother-in-law at 11:30 A.M. at Spence Manor and wanted to look sharp. She shouted to Bill, who was reading in bed, "Honey, I'll be out on some errands. Are you going out for your golf lesson?"

"Yeah."

"Good."

Linda picked up her purse and called into the bedroom, "Don't go back to sleep. When the maid comes, tell her to save that newspaper. There's something in it I want to read. And pick up your suit at the Oxford Shop. I want you to wear it to church Sunday."

"Okay."

Linda Zephries sat on a small chair in the suite of Rosanna Zephries. She had absentmindedly slipped a foot from her shoe and wiggled her toes in the plush carpet. Rosanna stood by the window and looked out over downtown Nashville. Linda was surprised at how small and trim she looked after the stories she had heard and the description Philip had given of her. Linda thought her to be an attractive and almost elegant woman.

Rosanna was dressed in a pair of gray slacks, a black silk blouse, a silver belt, and a light blue scarf tied casually about her neck. Rosanna spoke to the window. "So you want to restore the old place?"

She had spoken in a voice that was void of any trace of a southern accent. She spoke in quiet tones even though the monologue was bitter. "There was a day or two in the past week that I would have preferred to see it burned."

She turned from the window and took a seat at a desk that was cluttered with the contents from a large briefcase that sat on the floor. "Excuse this mess, but business goes on even when life takes a turn."

Linda matched the tone of the conversation, "I understand that."

The phone rang and Rosanna picked it up. "Hello." She sat with a calm expression on her smooth, dark-complexioned face. "Let me get back to you in a few minutes. I have someone with me at the moment."

Linda Zephries fidgeted slightly as the woman turned from the phone at looked at her a full five seconds with a blank expression on her face. Linda broke the silence. "If you have something to do, I can wait in the other room."

Rosanna Zephries rubbed her eyes as if she had been daydreaming. "Oh, no, it's quite all right. I would like to get some paperwork together. Could we meet again Friday? I just need a day or two, and I have to change some plans."

"Well, of course. Friday is fine."

"Good."

Rosanna went back to the window and spoke with her back turned. "It could be beautifully restored, you know. It's a grand old house."

Til was upstairs making beds and gathering laundry when she heard a car pull up outside. She heard the kitchen door slam and Linda calling her name. She went to the head of the stairs. "I'se up here. What you want? Quit slammin' dem doas like dat."

Linda leaned around the corner and smiled up the stairs. "Okay, if you don't want to hear the latest news, just stay up there."

Til came tromping down the stairs carrying an armload of bedclothes. "I'se fixin' to come down anyway. What you got yo'self into now?"

"Make a cup of coffee for us and sit down."

"If this is sittin' down news, I ain't too sho' I wanna hear it."

"Oh, it's good news. We don't have to move. We can stay here. Right here in this house."

Til turned from where she was making coffee. "Shut yo' mouf, girl. Tell me you just kiddin'."

"It's true, Til. I had a meeting with Rosanna this morning,

and I think she's going to sell this place to me."

Til frowned and folded her arms across her stomach. "Bill know 'bout dis?"

"No."

"You crazy, girl. He gonna blow his stack when he find out you talking to dat woman behind his back. What she like?"

Linda got up and walked to the kitchen window. She turned and put her hands on her hips. "She's just a woman who knows what she wants. And I'm a woman who knows what she wants."

Til poured the coffee and spoke without looking up. "I don't know what you two women wants, but I got a feeling I know what you gonna get when Bill find out."

Linda put her hand to her chin and squinted her eyes. "There'll be a time and a way to tell him. I can handle that. It's not final. We're going to meet again Friday. She wants to get some papers together."

Til stared into her coffee cup. "I swear y'all gonna make a old woman outta me yet."

Linda waved her hand as if to brush away the problem. "You're already an old woman, and you don't want to lose this place anymore than I do."

"Well, I ain't near as old as I wanna be one way or another."

Gorman Weeds sat in the floor of one of the apartments he had been wiring for electricity. He usually stayed in one of the apartments where he was working. There was no furniture, but he liked the smell of the new carpet and fresh paint in these virgin domiciles. He carried a bedroll, a box of shaving gear, instant coffee, small necessities, and camped out where he worked when he could.

Gorman was an excellent electrician. He usually worked alone and had a way of getting into his work and getting lost in it. The kind of finished wiring he did required neatness. He seldom got a complaint, and there was more work available than he could do. He acquired his skill and served his apprenticeship with a now retired plumber and electrician who lived in Franklin. The plumber had been born in Spring Hill and was a big football fan.

As the evening was chilly, Gorman had turned on the oven in the kitchen stove and sat with his back to the kitchen doorframe sipping from a bottle of whiskey.

He took a picture from the old cardboard box that contained his personal belongings. It showed a young Sally Weeds jumping into the air as a cheerleader for the Spring Hill Raiders. It was his favorite picture of his ex-wife. He leaned over and propped the picture against the opposite doorframe. He sat and stared at it.

It bothered Gorman that no one understood his love for Sally. Sure, he had slapped her around a little. Women were supposed to like that. His father had told him just that thing: "Slap 'em around a little once in a while, and they'll know who's boss."

Gorman took a long drink from the bottle. He wiped his mouth and clenched his fist. He refrained from slamming the fist into the freshly painted wall. Once, when he had done that, the contractor on the job had wanted him to pay for the damage.

He had turned on all the lights in the two-bedroom apartment. He got up and walked through the rooms admiring his work. He flipped light switches on and off, he checked closet lights and flipped the lights on and off under the kitchen cabinets that lined the walls above the sink.

His mind, however, was far away, thinking of ways to kill Bill Zephries. He wanted it to be a thing he could do alone. Muff and Puff were unreliable and nervous. He had a terrible time with them after he shot at the man he thought was Bill Zephries. He was also shaken to find that Sally knew it was he who had done the shooting. She had not mentioned Muff or Puff, and so he felt safe that was over and done with, and the man had not been hurt anyway. Just scared the hell out of some real estate hunter. Now his mother was saying that Sally was blaming him for the fire in her trailer. Hell, he had not even been near Spring Hill when that happened. In fact, he had told her on occasion that the dammed old trailer was a firetrap and had offered to wire it properly for her. But, no, she thought it was just another approach to old times.

Walking the floors of the apartment, Gorman Weeds devised a plan. He would follow Bill Zephries until the time and place was right. Gorman took another long drink of whiskey from the bottle. Even if they caught him, it would be better than life without Sally. The notion of Bill Zephries being dead gave Gorman a sense of elation. Dead, gone, no more, out of here, history. He loved the thought and drank to it. He could pick a time and place. It had to be perfect. As perfect as the wiring job he had just finished in the apartment in which he contemplated murder.

Rosanna was not even mildly surprised when Sherman called and invited her to dinner at his apartment. "I'm not much of a cook," she had said.

Sherman laughed at the remark. "Let me assure you,

madame, that I'm not either. But let me surprise you. When can you come?"

"Eight is fashionable, isn't it?"

"Eight it is. I have the Mallory Suite on the top floor. And before you ask, I have no idea how it got such a name."

"See you at eight. Should I bring anything?"

Sherman paused. "No, no, just try to be on time."

Rosanna dressed in comfortable clothes and added some color to the outfit as a gesture of good nature. She had several things she wanted to know about her family that Sherman could tell her.

The elevator operator bowed and greeted Rosanna Zephries with, "Good evening, Mrs. Zephries."

It surprised the wary woman. She came to the conclusion that she was not the first lady to have dinner with the distinguished counselor in the Mallory Suite.

Rosanna Zephries was a well-trained saleslady. She had visited many suites, apartments, boathouses, yachts, and country homes in search of real estate deals. Never certain of her motives, she learned not to question them. Sure, she had slept with some of the right men in some of the right places when it was convenient for business. But had she not enjoyed the majority of the trysts? Wasn't she selective and discreet?

Buoyed by her past conquests, Rosanna smiled broadly and almost giggled when Sherman answered her knock at the suite with a bow and a sweeping gesture to enter. "Why, Sherman, how gracious of you. Ain't this fun?"

Sherman Cooper was dressed in jeans, a pair of cowboy boots, and a red western shirt. Rosanna looked him up and down and exclaimed, "Oh, mercy, am I overdressed?"

"No, of course not." Sherman pantomimed the drawing of two six-shooters from imaginary holsters. "These are my work clothes."

Rosanna laughed. "Oh, yes. You are a trail rider, aren't you?"

"Ma'am, you got that plumb right. I'm a real pilgrim of the dusty trail. Hey! Speaking of dusty, how 'bout a drink?"

"Thank you. Orange juice and vodka, if you have it." Amanda removed her light jacket and dropped it across the back of a chair. "My, what a nice place you have here. I'm glad you didn't clutter it with too much furniture. It has a spacious look as it is."

Sherman mixed drinks. "Thank you. But to tell you the truth it's pretty much the way I found it. I had those shelves put in for my books, and a friend of mine gave me that gun rack and that shotgun. I think of it as decoration."

The two settled in chairs across from one another. Rosanna looked around the room and said pleasantly, "I don't smell any food cooking. Don't tell me you ordered pizza?"

"Quite the contrary. Our dinner should arrive in thirty minutes or so."

"Something light, I hope."

"Uh, light but substantial. Do you like veal Oscar?"

"Yes, that would be just right."

"Well, just be patient."

Rosanna surveyed the room again. It was much too dark for her taste. Fine oak furniture; blue carpet that was antiqued either by time or design, she couldn't tell which with what little light was available; terracotta-colored leather chairs; tongue-and-groove oak flooring in the small entrance hall; landscape paintings and a sizeable portrait of Andrew Jackson on the walls. The doors to the kitchen and the bedrooms were closed.

Sherman Cooper took notice of the survey and added to her guesses. "There's good natural light in the kitchen through those double doors, and a generous window in the bedroom. I'm afraid it's all a bit masculine for such fine company."

"What sort of view do you have?"

"Uh, First Street and the Cumberland River."

"Good."

Sherman stood and went to the little brass-topped oak bar. "Want another?"

"Yes, please, that was very good. Maybe a little more ice."

"Coming up."

Rosanna stood and walked toward the portrait of Andrew Jackson. She stopped and turned, standing just under the portrait, as if comparing herself to the painting. "What are my boys like, Sherman?"

The tall, gray gentleman handed her the drink. "Oh, I guess they are boys as boys will be boys. That sort of thing."

"That implies some vices, doesn't it?"

"Well, yes, I guess you could say that."

Rosanna dug in. "What kind of vices? Tell me now. You're not in this thing anymore. I'm not a client. I'd rather you'd think of me as a friend."

"Well, certainly. I surely believe that after all these years."

Rosanna put her hands behind her neck and shook her hair as if relaxing for a long evening. "What kinds of vices?"

"They're not gay," he laughed.

"Yes?"

"Bill smokes, you know."

"Yes?"

"Well, stuff like that . . . uh, you know."

"I'm not digging. I'm just curious."

"Well, look, this is only rumor, off the street, lunch-at-Printers-Alley-type talk . . ." Sherman mixed his drink. "Look, I don't want this to be our dinner conversation, so I'll tell you this. I think Bill is doing cocaine."

"Cocaine?"

Sherman shrugged it off. "Bill always drank and raised hell, but this coke thing is something else."

168

"I know what you mean. Do you think it's bad?"

"Not now. Not yet. Who knows?"

"Phillip?"

"I don't know Phillip that well. He was at MTSU, then St. Louis. He's a nice kid though. Kind of a dreamer, but a nice boy."

"Thank you."

"Not at all. He's a nice young man."

"No, I mean thanks for telling me about Bill. I'm not sure I wanted to know. But thank you." Rosanna sipped her drink. "Linda's having a baby."

"I didn't know you knew."

"Women suspect."

"You tricked me. You didn't know."

Sherman Cooper turned and started back to his chair. He wobbled a bit and then caught his balance. "Whoops, I guess I'm not used to these boots. I only wear them once or twice a year, barbecue outing or something like that."

He settled in his chair and glanced at his watch. "Dinner should be here soon. Hungry?"

"Yes," Rosanna said, taking her chair again.

When the food came, Sherman explained that a client of his owned a restaurant not far away, and it was an exchange of courtesies that he was afforded a dinner like this on occasion.

The young man who brought the food in portable, metal containers helped himself to china and silverware from the kitchen. He wheeled out a table and two chairs from the kitchen, produced a white linen tablecloth, lit a candle, and poured the wine. Rosanna Zephries sat nodding her approval at a pleased Sherman Cooper.

There was veal Oscar, a bibb lettuce salad, honey-mustard dressing, hard rolls, broccoli with cheese, green beans with almonds, and a chocolate mousse.

Sherman patted his mouth with his napkin and explained the menu. "I usually order what I like and then hope."

Rosanna smacked her lips at the mousse and smiled. "Clever of you not to order potatoes for a lady and then have this vicious chocolate."

When they finished dinner, Sherman pushed the table back toward the kitchen and offered an after-dinner drink. "I have some good brandy, or perhaps a liqueur?"

"Nothing for me, thank you."

Rosanna stood and walked toward the portrait of Andrew Jackson again. "You know, Sherman, this is the way it should be. I mean, civilized people being civilized." She turned to the tall old man who stood behind the bar pouring brandy. "It was very nice of you to invite me here and to share with me. Your fantasy," she laughed, "and such."

Sherman came from behind the bar. "There's one piece of business about, but . . ." He reached to a shelf behind his chair and produced a small velvet box and handed it to Rosanna. "This was in her lockbox. I couldn't figure out why she had kept it all these years. It appears to be almost worthless, but your name is on a bracelet."

Rosanna took the small box and looked at it in awe. She opened it to see several pairs of cheap earrings, a brass bracelet, and a gold-plated chain with a small gold cross attached. She looked up from the box and stared at the wall for a moment. She laughed, "My God, she didn't even give Til this worthless little box of trinkets I left. She cut me out completely. This is how absolutely she wanted me out of their lives. It's amazing. Amazing!"

The woman paced the room as she spoke. You know something, Sherman, I'm alive. I'm alive. My sons are alive, my daughter-in-law is alive, and the Old Zephries Place is still standing." She turned to stare at her white-haired host. "Do you see that? I'm alive."

Sherman Cooper flinched as Rosanna Zephries laughed aloud. "Know what I'd like to do? Give Til this box of jewelry. I wanted her to have it. And give my daughter-in-law the Old Zephries Place. I'd have everything I've always wanted. My children, my grandchildren, and the great satisfaction of knowing that all the days of my young life were not wasted in trying to help my children."

Sherman Cooper mumbled something Rosanna did not hear. "What?" she asked.

Sherman said, "I don't believe I would continue a war with a dead woman. Amanda Zephries is dead."

Rosanna picked up her coat and the small box and walked to the door of the suite. She turned and spoke with finality. "Sherman, in law there are no dead and buried adversaries; in life there are. Good night, and thanks for a wonderful evening."

CHAPTER TWELVE

SUMMERTIME AND EASY LIVING

Linda Zephries made sure that Bill was still asleep when she dialed Rosanna from the kitchen phone. She spoke in a low voice and let Rosanna know that Bill was in the apartment. It was a chatty conversation. The two women were bound by their common affection for Bill Zephries, the coming babies, and the Old Zephries Place. It was a cool alliance, but an alliance nonetheless. Both women urged the other to further and further revelations of their lives. Linda made jokes of Bill's eccentricities; Rosanna shared a few stories about the days when she mothered two children without benefit of indoor plumbing. It was the first occasion in Nashville that Rosanna had found to make light of her earlier plight. If the bitter humor was lost on Linda, it was a burden lifted from the mind of the mother-in-law.

Linda made known her plans to renovate and restore the old house and grounds. Rosanna joined in enthusiastically, although she did refrain from mentioning her own ill-fated plans to glorify her tainted past with just such restoration. The sadness of the conversation was Rosanna's growing knowledge that the dream had been passed into younger, and perhaps more capable, hands.

Linda pressed for numbers and sales figures concerning the real estate in question. Rosanna good-naturedly shunned the questions and kept reaffirming an appointment they had made for that afternoon at one o'clock. Finally Linda bluntly asked, "How much money are we talking about, Rosanna? How much?"

Rosanna said, "You just be here at one. I might have a pleasant surprise for you."

The two women closed their phone conversation by agreeing that brighter days were ahead for the Zephries.

Linda Zephries hung up the phone and lit a cigarette. She looked at the kitchen clock. It was nine-fifteen.

Bill came down the hallway from the bedroom, "What's wrong with our TV?"

"I don't know. I think it's the cable company again. They go blank once in a while."

"We need a regular TV here. Hell, we live right in the middle of town. We don't need cable that bad."

"Quit yelling and come in here if you want to talk. I can't shout." Bill went silent. Linda poured herself another cup of coffee. She was dressed in jeans, a floppy white shirt hanging over her midriff, and a pale blue jacket thrown over her shoulders.

Bill came into the kitchen wearing his pajama bottoms. He yawned and stretched. Linda handed him a cup of coffee as he went to the window and pulled back the louvered blinds. "What's the weather like out there? Looks pretty good for golf."

"Are you golfing again?"

"Yeah."

"Nice day for it."

Bill sat down at the kitchen table and flipped the pages of the *Tennessean*. "You know what I'd like to do one of these days?"

"What?"

"Go fishing."

"Fishing?"

"Yeah, catfishing. Go down to the old Duck River, build a fire on the bank, dig some worms, cook some hot dogs, and catch some fish. I want to teach my boys how to fish. What do you think?"

"I think you're crazy. You don't know yet if they're boys. Besides, the bugs would eat me alive on a riverbank at night."

"Aw, you can use that spray stuff to keep bugs away."

"I'm allergic to that stuff too."

"Well, we could buy us a boat and fish the lake."

"What lake?"

"Any lake, Old Hickory, Percy Priest, any lake we please."

"What's wrong with you? I never knew you were so big on the great outdoors."

Bill sipped the coffee and smiled. "You know, when Phillip and me was kids we practically lived in the woods and on the riverbank."

"Well, maybe Phillip would like to live in the woods, but I wouldn't."

Bill stood and went back to the window. "Ever eat fried rabbit?"

Linda made a face. "Fried rabbit? Lord, no!"

"Probably my all-time favorite food, fried rabbit."

"What's got into you this morning?"

"Nothing. I just like getting out in the country, that's all."

Linda watched her husband's back for a moment. She saw an opportunity in the conversation. She said, "Bill?"

"Yes."

"Uh, what do you think of the Old Zephries Place?"

Bill scratched his head. "I don't think about it at all. Why do you ask?"

"You think it could be restored?"

"Anything can be restored, I guess. Why?"

"I was just thinking. That's all."

Bill Zephries frowned. He opened his mouth and started to say something, then changed his mind.

Linda rinsed her coffee cup and put it away. "Well, at least he didn't do a flip," she thought.

Bill lit a cigarette. "How is the decorating going at the condo? You get the nursery painted yet?"

"They'll do that sometime this week."

"They're supposed to be finished by now, ain't they?"

"Aren't they."

"That's what I said."

"You said 'ain't.'"

"I'm putting you on."

Bill sat back down at the small kitchen table. "I'll be glad to get out of here. This place is starting to get on my nerves."

"Why?"

"Well, in the first place it's your apartment. I'd like to get some of my stuff out of storage and have it where I can find it."

Linda bent over and kissed him on the top of the head. "I know, I know. It won't be long."

Linda leafed through a magazine on the countertop and spoke casually. "Bill, do you know anything about the history of Spring Hill and Maury County?"

Bill looked up smiled. "Yeah, it used to be a hole in the ground, and now it's a hole in the wall."

"Seriously. It has a great history. Do you know that Lewis of Lewis and Clark is buried over there near the Natchez Trace?"

"No. Do you mean the expedition guys?"

"Yes, Meriwether Lewis is buried in Lewis County, which used to be a part of Maury. There's some mystery about how he died. He was on his way from St. Louis to Washington and was traveling the old Natchez Trace when it happened. When the Tennessee State Legislature decided to put up a monument for him in 1848, they had to dig around until they found a grave that had homemade nails in the coffin. A man named Cooper had forged the nails, and so he went out there and identified the nails and so found the grave of Lewis."

"I remember reading about the expedition. That's about it."

"They never found the gold he was supposed to be carrying with him. Some people suspected that he was robbed and murdered when he stopped off at a wilderness hotel called Grinder's Stand. There was an old black lady over in there by the name of Aunt Melindy. She said when she was a little girl she heard gunshots and saw Lewis staggering around bleeding and begging for water. I don't think many historians bought the story, but it was a real mystery, and still is."

"You're really into that history business, ain't you?"

"You don't have to be an historian to appreciate a man like that. He was once Thomas Jefferson's private secretary and held the governorship of Louisiana at the time of his death."

"It seems to me he would have been more important if he lived here instead of dying here."

"Well, if you would read some of the history of the area you would appreciate it more. Nathan Bedford Forrest killed a man named Wills Gould with a penknife in Columbia. Gould shot Forrest in the leg."

"It must have happened while the TV was on the blink. I missed it."

Linda frowned. "You're impossible."

Bill took her into his arms and kissed the top of her head. "Look, it's gotta be spring fever or something. You're hung up on history today, and I'm hung up on a catfish line. What say we don't start an argument?"

Linda laughed. "You're right. I don't have time to argue anyway. I've got woman things to do. Go on and play golf."

"You goin' out?"

"Yes. I should be back in the afternoon early."

"Well, I might not see you anymore today. If I finish at the club in time, I'll stop by for awhile. I've got that meeting tonight."

"How late will you be?"

"I don't know, but don't wait up. I've got my key."

"Don't stay out all night with those tobacco people." Linda shook her finger at him.

Bill Zephries looked lovingly at her. "I love all three of you guys."

"We love you too, but you still must come home at a decent hour. Bye."

Bill Zephries went back to the bedroom and lay down on the floor by the bed. He reached under the bed and retrieved a small black briefcase. He flipped the latches on the briefcase, and the lid sprang open to reveal a neat stack of one-hundred-dollar bills in gold wrappers, fifty thousand dollars in all. Bill visually determined that the money was all there. He closed the briefcase and put it on the bed. He sat down on the bed and lit a cigarette.

The money in the briefcase was part of a plan Bill Zephries had formulated to simplify his cocaine buying. He had been paying a hundred dollars or more for a small packet. His plan was to buy fifty thousand dollars' worth at a bargain price.

The young man considered cocaine to be his salvation. It made him socially comfortable, it made him daring in business, and it kept him calm in crises. He felt that he needed it, and he definitely wanted it.

Bill puffed on the cigarette and mused on his plans. After all, he was on the verge of building an empire. He could see himself in the future as being the owner of the most modern tobacco warehouse in middle Tennessee. He had sold tobacco for years, and there were a million things they were doing wrong. Maury County tobacco farmers usually took their crops to the Jewell tobacco warehouse in Franklin or the Columbia tobacco warehouse. There would be no need for that when he had built his warehouse. He would also show Linda that he could be a businessman alongside the best of them. He slapped his open palm across his leg in anticipation of his conquest.

It was a dangerous project to buy coke in Nashville or Columbia. Police knew or suspected most dealers, and a man of Bill Zephries's reputation could not be seen in such areas, if he had not been seen already.

He had some trouble negotiating the deal to buy the coke. But being an old tobacco and horse trader, he had gotten a bargain deal on what he considered a lifetime supply. He intended to quit using it as soon as he was free of the pressure of building his tobacco warehouse.

The man had told him that the transaction would take place in an open field at night. Bill didn't understand why he couldn't pick it up downtown. He also didn't understand when the man said it had to be done outside cowboy territory. He had been warned that others knew about the deal and that the money had to be unmarked, untraceable, and in one-hundred-dollar bills. Any slip-ups and there could be dire consequences.

Bill Zephries reached his hand between the mattresses on the bed where he sat planning his future. He removed a small packet and did some cocaine. He had decided that it also improved his golf swing, and he was meeting some very competitive friends at the country club at noon.

Gorman Weeds was trying to borrow his boss's truck. "Look, Ed, I just need it for a few days while they put a clutch in my old Plymouth."

The man turned and looked Gorman in the eye. He had heard a lot of stories from this man and was always suspicious of his motives. "What's wrong with the clutch? You drove it over here, didn't you?"

"Slips real bad. Could go any minute. I don't wanna get stuck away from the job."

"You know I don't loan company trucks."

"Alfred used one the other day."

"That was an emergency."

"This is too."

The old contractor spit into the dust at his feet. "How near you finished on that Brett street project?"

"Got seventeen rooms to do."

The contractor was impressed. He took off his glasses and tapped them on his hand. "Take that blue Chevy, have it back by Friday, and you can't drive it on the weekend."

"I'd rather have that black Ford with the V8. That damned Chevy won't pull a marshmallow off a cup of hot chocolate."

The contractor was surprised since the Chevy was a newer truck. "Okay, take the Ford, but check the oil in it."

"Right. Thank you."

"Friday."

"Right."

Gorman got into the pickup and started the engine. It roared. He leaned out the window and shouted at the boss, "Hey, Ed, think we oughta put a muffler on this son of a bitch?"

"Just drive it and let me worry about the muffler."

Gorman shrugged his shoulders. "Okay."

Later that day, Gorman patched the muffler. He would need a plain, quiet, black vehicle to tail Bill Zephries. The old Ford would be perfect.

In Spring Hill, Tennessee, the bluebirds made their way to the holes they could find in old wooden fence posts and similar abodes. They darted back and forth to their nests-in-progress with a dedication that General Motors had envied in the Japanese. The flags waved in the breeze over the site of Saturn. A guard at the gate to the massive expanse of land shook his head to stay awake in the warm sunshine and occasionally waved a truck or automobile through the gate. Work at the site seemed to ease along as if time were of no consequence. Residents of the area had somehow expected the multi-billion dollar plant to rise from the ground like a hot-air balloon. Once plans had been made and decisions had been hammered into action, construction assumed its own pace. Men stood drinking soft drinks and eating candy bars as others strung lines of twine and stakes along mysteriously shaped borders. Each had his own set of plans laid across the hoods of pickup trucks and Cadillacs. Occasionally a helicopter would arrive at the site blowing dust and gravel over the area. Men in suits and ties would emerge and stand gesturing and pointing to different areas of the once lush pasture land. The bluebirds would pause momentarily as the helicopter rose into the air and disappeared into the distance. The bluebirds had a schedule ordained by a power higher than that of General Motors.

Widow Weeds was talking to her friend on the telephone. "Thelma, they got any onion sets down at the co-op yet?"

"I don't think so. They're always a little later than the hardware store. Might be some there though. You getting garden fever?"

"I always put in a little something. Seems like less and less ever' year to me. I can't get straightened up once I get bent over any more. Old age, I reckon."

"You hear from Gorman?"

"Said he'd be over here today to get that ol' black jumpsuit outta his closet. I keep his things washed up for him. Don't know what he wants with that thing. He always said he hated it cause it binded him in the crotch so much. He's lost some weight though. I don't know what he eats. I told him to come on home and stay in his own room for a while. He said he's just about finished with that job over there by Hickory Hollow. I wish he'd just come on home and let me put some meat on his bones. Lord, I worry about him though."

"I reckon."

"What's going on over at your place?"

"Well, they loaded up the trash left over from Sally's trailer fire and hauled it off. Ain't nothing over there but a big black spot now."

"Wonder where she's living."

"Beats me. She didn't stay in that trailer much anyway. Just came by now and then to change clothes if you ask me."

"Is the Zephries moved out of that old place yet?"

"They moving. That colored woman Til who worked up there dug up a bunch of flower bushes and hauled 'em over there to a friend's place on Duplex. They're just sitting out there in the back yard. They'll die off 'fore she gets 'em in the ground, I guess."

"How'd you know about that?"

"Mavis lives right up there behind 'em. She saw it."

Widow Weeds leaned toward the window and saw Gorman pull into the drive in a black pickup truck. She spoke into the phone hurriedly, "I'll call you back, Thelma. Gorman's here."

Gorman Weeds banged the screen door as he entered the house. His mother called to him, "Hi, honey."

Gorman hugged his mother and kissed her cheek. "How you feeling? Okay?"

"I feel tolerable, I guess. Arthritis don't get no better or worse, I reckon. Can I fix you a bite?"

"You can fix me a bologna sandwich if you want to. Put some mayonnaise on it."

Widow Weeds scoffed. "Lord, I reckon I know how you like your bologna sandwiches by now. I been fixin' 'em long enough. You want milk?"

"Yeah." Gorman followed his mother into the kitchen and sat down at the table. "Any news around here to speak of?"

"No, just the same old stuff—Saturn, Saturn, Saturn."

"They hiring anybody?"

"Not a soul that I know of."

"Sally find a place to stay?"

"I don't know if she did or not, and Thelma don't either. They cleaned up that place where her trailer was. Hauled it off."

"Zephries move out yet?"

"They're moving now. Dug up some flower bushes to take with 'em, wherever they going."

"Wonder if they're gonna move them graves on the place."

Widow Weeds turned from the stove and placed one hand on her hip. "Now that's a good question. Reckon they'll just leave 'em there for the Japs to pour concrete over? Or maybe that Rosanna woman will dig 'em up and spit in their eye."

"I wouldn't be surprised what they did. Put some onion on that sandwich too."

"Okay, honey." She paused at the kitchen counter and

turned to the young man sprawled in the chair. "What have you been up to, honey?"

Gorman shrugged. "Aw, nothin'." In fact, he had been following Bill Zephries around Nashville for the past few days. He had watched the young man-about-town play golf, go nightclubbing, shop for clothes, and for some quirky reason make a lot of calls from pay phones.

After eating the sandwich, Gorman Weeds went to the bedroom and wrapped a rifle in his old black jumpsuit and kissed his mother good-bye.

CHAPTER THIRTEEN

WHERE DO I SIGN?

Linda Zephries drove warily toward Spence Manor where
Rosanna waited. The afternoon traffic was heavy and she
sensed a feeling of protection of her babies. She wasn't sure of
the feeling, but it was new to her and she examined it closely
in her mind. The radio was tuned to a local talk show. A man
had phoned in to talk about Saturn coming to Spring Hill. He
spoke in a rural country voice and spoke boldly. "Well, I told
my mama when I was a little boy that I wasn't going to
Detroit or nowhere else for a job. I told my daddy, too. I said
from the very first that I was gonna stay here in my hometown
and make a living even if I had to pick up pop bottles to do it.
Ever since I was a little kid all people ever did was graduate
from high school, grab a suitcase, and take off for a factory job.
I said, well, when I grow up I'm staying right here in good old
Spring Hill. They'd go off and work a while and then come
back with a big old Chevy with white wall tires, and there'd be
two or three kids hanging out the window, and they'd stay two
or three days on the Fourth of July or something and then
they'd head right back to Detroit or Columbus or Mansfield or
someplace, and go right back to work in them factories. Well, I
make a darn good living hauling pulpwood and firewood and
never asked nobody for nothing, and one day I look around and
they building one of them damned factories right in my back

door, and I said to hell with this, and I sold out and I'm moving south. That's my idea of it."

The announcer broke in and said, "Thank you for calling. We gotta go. Thank you."

Linda turned off the radio and adjusted her extra weight in the seat of the car. She turned into the Spence Manor parking lot, lit a cigarette, and noted the time as being 12:50 P.M., a little early for her appointment with Rosanna Zephries.

She sat smoking the cigarette when a big black Cadillac pulled into the parking place alongside her. She glanced toward the car and saw a man wearing a red-flowered cowboy shirt and a big western hat. She leaned toward the ashtray and tapped her cigarette in it, then she quickly jerked her head back toward the Cadillac. "My God, that's Sherman Cooper," she said aloud.

The old counselor closed his car door and walked past her toward the door of Spence Manor. Linda rolled the car window down and shouted, "Hey, cowboy, where you headed?"

Sherman Cooper turned and peered toward the girl. He was not wearing his glasses. "That you, Linda?" He fished in his brightly colored shirt pocket and found his glasses and placed them on his nose. "How are you?"

Linda stepped from her car. "What are you up to in that costume?" The old man looked down at his cowboy boots. "It's a long story. Let's go on up."

"Where are you going?"

"To see Rosanna. Isn't that where you're going?"

"Well, yes. But I didn't know you were coming."

Sherman switched his briefcase to his other hand. "Oh, well, she'll tell us why we're here, I guess. Come on."

The two entered the lobby of Spence Manor. Linda looked curiously at Sherman's wardrobe as they rode the elevator to Rosanna's suite.

Rosanna answered the knock at her door and ushered the

two into the large sitting room. She seemed nervous. "Coffee, drinks, can I get you anything?"

Sherman accepted coffee. Linda declined and sat perched on the edge of a straight-backed chair with her purse dangling toward the floor on its leather strap. She looked like a visiting teen-aged niece.

Rosanna sipped orange juice as she stood in the center of the room. Sherman reclined in a comfortable chair. Rosanna seemed to take sudden notice of Sherman's clothes. "My Lord, Sherman, you look awesome in that outfit."

"Yes, I do, don't I?"

Rosanna pulled a chair toward the center of the room and sat down. Sherman opened his briefcase and started taking papers from it. Linda sat back farther in her chair. She spoke with some hesitation. "Would someone explain my tension?" She managed a small, nervous chuckle.

Rosanna Zephries looked at Sherman. "I'll let you explain it, Sherman. Go ahead."

Sherman sat upright and spoke jovially. "Well, looks like I get to play cowboy and Santa Claus in the same day. Linda, the bad news is that the Old Zephries Place is not for sale. The good news is, Rosanna is going to give it to you." He paused before adding, "If you want it."

Linda looked first at one member of the group and then the other. Her eyes settled on Rosanna. "Why? We can afford to buy it."

Sherman Cooper looked sternly at Linda. He spoke in his best lawyer's voice. "Linda, look. Her husband is buried there. The grandfather of her children is buried there. Her children were conceived and born there. You have to understand that. Rosanna has as much regard for the Old Zephries Place as you."

Linda pursed her lips and tapped her index finger to her forehead. "Yes, of course. I know."

Sherman Cooper continued. "It's simple. The house and the ten acres are for you, Bill, Phillip, and any grandchildren. The place will truly belong to the Zephries, and Rosanna won't have any involvement once these papers are signed."

The room was quiet. Linda said, "Let me see the papers." She sat reading for a few minutes. She turned the small, three-page document over in her hands. "Is this all of it?"

Sherman held out some other papers. "This is the deed."

Linda looked at Rosanna. "You won't sell?"

Rosanna averted her stare and looked out the window at the beautiful day. "No, no, I couldn't do that. I spent too many years trying to get the property back into the hands of my children. This is a God-given opportunity to do that." She looked at Linda. "I was so happy when you showed concern for the place. You have an understanding of such things. Sherman tells me you are an historian. That's wonderful. That's exactly the kind of attitude the place needs. You know it's made of solid lumber, and the foundation is laid on rock. It could be made into a real showplace. You can afford it, and you can do it. You have the talent and the love. I do hope you'll take it."

Linda said, "Do you think Bill will accept it?"

Rosanna said, "When I'm gone back to California he will." "And Phillip?"

Sherman said, "Phillip will do whatever will make everybody happy." Linda got up and walked toward the window. "If this is the only way to keep the old place, and I guess it is, I couldn't bear to turn it down." She turned quickly and added, "Oh, I sound ungrateful, Rosanna, but I didn't mean to. It's just that so much has happened. I heard a man on the radio a few minutes ago talking about Saturn and it depressed me. I mean, what has General Motors done wrong? You'd think they came here as carpetbaggers or something. It seems to me that they made a monumental effort to assuage the feelings of the local folks. They knew Spring Hill was no metropolis. I just wish the governor had handled the public relations a little better. All that ignoring Spring Hill as he tried to do. I know he thought of it as a Tennessee project, but this is a big state. People in Knoxville could care less if they build a plant in Spring Hill. I think people can sense that the economy is really a national if not an international business. Oh, I'm sorry. Guess I'll get off my soapbox. By golly, let's do it!"

"My God, do you mean to tell me that you made a deal for a whole friggin' house, and from my mother to boot, without even talkin' to me?" Bill threw his coffee cup through a glassed-in china cabinet door. He called his mother vile names and screamed at his wife. He really knew little of the agreement other than the fact that his mother was giving the property to them.

In fact, Bill himself had thought of finding a way to get his hands on the Old Zephries Place, but he had wanted to buy it, perhaps from the Japanese. He really felt he could buy anything he wanted now, and it frustrated him to know that he had been out-maneuvered.

When he calmed down and Linda had cried a few appropriate tears, he signed the deed transfer and threw it to the floor at Linda's feet. He was still angry when he spoke. "There, I've signed the damned thing. I don't want to hear any more about it. Do what you please with it. I still don't see why we couldn't have bought the damned place."

Linda quietly picked up the paper from the floor and laid it on the kitchen countertop. She nervously poured her husband another cup of coffee. Bill sipped the coffee and kicked the broken glass from under his feet with his sneaker. He looked at his wife standing motionless at the counter. "Look, I'm not sorry, but . . . well, yes, I am sorry. Sorry that bitch . . . I'm sorry that woman ever came back to this town. I'm sorry about that." He sipped his coffee. "One thing. We won't have to move the graves. I was worried about what to do about that. They can stay there."

Linda turned and said, "I'm going to put up proper markers and have the place fenced and landscaped, if you'll let me."

Bill looked at her and nodded. "That'd be nice. It should be done."

"I want to turn it into a place you'll be proud of. We could have summer visits there. A summer place. We could have friends out."

Bill got up from his chair and said abruptly, "I've got that meeting tonight. It's important. I don't know exactly what time I'm gonna get in."

He walked toward the bedroom, kicking glass. He turned at the bedroom door and said, "Better call, or better yet, go see Phillip and tell him he doesn't have to pack and run." Bill scratched his chin. "He'll be glad to know the place is back in the family. He's a sentimental son of a bitch."

Linda Zephries dialed the Old Zephries Place. Til answered the phone. "Zephries residence."

"Til, this is Linda. Is Phillip there?"

"I don't know if he here or no. How much money you got? I charges to talk to him, you know."

"Til, this is important. I need to talk to him."

"Well, now, important or what, I still charges fifty cents to talk to the boss man." Til laughed. "He upstairs. I'll holler at him."

Linda stood with the phone to her ear. She could hear Til talking up the stairs. "He say he'll call you right back. You at home?"

"Tell him I want to come out and see him if he's going to be there for a little while."

"Jest a minute."

Linda could hear more conversation by way of the stairs. Til came back to the phone. "He say come on out."

Linda drove the fifty-five mile per hour speed limit as she took I-65 toward Brentwood, Franklin, and out to the Spring Hill exit. She made note of the construction projects she saw along the way. It seemed the influence of Saturn was now a general boom and reached all the way to Nashville. The computers had cranked out their numbers for speculators, and it all added up to money. Interest rates were down, inflation was down, money was easy to borrow, and the weather was perfect for tearing down and building up.

Nearing the Maury county line, the large gracious farmhouses still stood. Cattle grazed in lush pastures. Trees were greening out all over, and birds, large and small, darted here and there in the bright sunshine as if the planet was theirs alone. Linda adjusted her weight in the seat of the car and tugged at the maternity jeans she was wearing. She was surprised at how fast her babies were growing and how aware she was becoming of these other people being always with her. It gave her a sense of permanence, a new religion made manifest in a single knowledge that she could not verbalize.

On entering the Spring Hill city limits, Linda kept driving. She stopped momentarily behind a school bus and noticed that the old crazy preacher Joseph Armes still had his station wagon and trailer parked by the roadside. She went past her turn to Sugar Ridge and kept driving out toward the Saturn site. When she reached the former Hayne's Haven Farm where the plant was now being laid out, she pulled to the left side of the road across from the guard house and entrance and sat looking at the flags. The American flag, Tennessee flag, and the General Motors banner waved side by side in the gentle breeze. She was surprised to see the glistening white fences that surrounded the place. There was no trash, no clumsy vehicles parked around, and no mud and dirt dragged out onto the Memorial Highway. It did, as they had said it would, look like the makings of a quiet college campus. She started to light a cigarette sitting there in the warm afternoon and suddenly realized, in full, that she was giving her children a cigarette. She threw the cigarette out the window and crumpled the pack in her hand.

She turned in the wide expanse of the road and drove back toward the Old Zephries Place.

Til was sitting on a stool watching a soap opera on TV and eating a sandwich. Linda looked around the kitchen. "Where's Phillip?"

"He upstairs. He be down in a minute."

"What are you watching?"

Til wiped her mouth with her hand. "Lawd, I don't know. I stopped by here a minute and this woman said she gonna give her baby to a communist farm 'cause her husband being held hostage someplace and her daddy is fixin' to have her put away and she don't know dat boy she thinks is a hostage is living right down the road a few miles with her sister, or something like dat. Lawd, these white folks is crazier on TV than dey is right here on earth."

Linda watched the TV for a second. She dropped her purse and a manila envelope of papers on a chair and said, "I'm going upstairs to use the bathroom."

Til could hear the stairs creaking as Linda took them carefully, one at a time. Til turned off the TV and stood at the sink and washed the dish and the glass she had been using.

Linda came back downstairs. "Do you leave your underwear lying around like that all the time?"

"What underwear?"

"In the bathroom."

"Lawd, dat ain't mine. Dat's Sally's. She leave everything all over wherever she drop it."

Linda frowned. "Better put it away. Someone might come by."

Til turned and snorted, "I ain't pickin' up after her. She ain't no business of mine. She full-grown, if you ask me."

"Where is she?"

"Went to the store. Said she gonna fix supper. Ain't feedin' me nothin'. I be 'fraid of poison."

There were footsteps on the stairs. Phillip walked into the kitchen and said, "Hello, you all." He kissed Linda on the cheek and said, "Did you bring the papers?"

Linda stood stunned for a moment. She turned to look at the chair where the papers lay, then turned back to Phillip, "You know?"

"Sherman called last night. He let me know in no uncertain terms he was representing Rosanna, but he apologized for going around you to me."

Linda stood silent and perplexed for a moment. Her whole rehearsed speech had been rendered useless. She said quietly, "Yes, I brought the papers."

"You get Bill to sign them?"

"Yes, but it wasn't easy." Linda handed him the envelope. "What do you think?"

"If it's on paper the way I heard it, I'll sign. I'd like to read it first."

Linda reached for a cigarette and stopped in midmotion. "Of course. I'd like to walk around outside a little bit while you read. I'm not sure I ever really looked at the place. It was in negotiation when I first saw it."

Phillip said, "Til, how 'bout a cup while I read this?"

"Uh huh."

Sherman Cooper drove his Cadillac into the gate of a big farm just off I-40 several miles east of Nashville. He turned into a grassy parking area beside a huge barn surrounded by corrals. Several horses inside the fences made note of his arrival by jerking their heads up and down. As Sherman stepped from the car, a small man in faded jeans, cowboy shirt, and scuffed cowboy boots came from inside the barn. "Howdy, Mister Cooper. Been expecting you."

"Good. Good." Sherman was opening the trunk of the car. "Got my horse ready?"

"Yes sir, she's all saddled up."

"She?" Sherman stood taken aback. "Is that horse a she?"

"Why, yes sir. Always has been."

Sherman Cooper shrugged his shoulders and started unloading the trunk of the car. "Well, bring her out here then. Bring her on out. What do you call her?"

"Well, sir, you can call her anything you want to now that she's yours."

Sherman thought for a minute. "I'll call her Lorraine. What do you think of that for a name for a horse?"

"Sounds fine, sir. They respond to a good distinctive name."

"Good. Bring old Lorraine out here then."

The young man went into the barn and came out leading a big red mare with a white mane. The horse walked ploddingly and easily at the shoulder of the small man. "Here she is, Mister Cooper."

Sherman looked up and smiled. "Howdy, Lorraine, old pal of mine." He took a drink from a bottle of Jack Daniels whiskey and lit a cigarette. "We going on a little trail ride, ol' gal." He took a harmonica from his shirt pocket and blew across the scale, making a riffling noise. He replaced the harmonica and looked at the gear he had piled up on the ground. He bent over and picked up a rifle scabbard. "Here, son, see if you can get this on that saddle somewhere. Here's a set of instructions on how it goes on." He handed the small man a white sheet of paper.

The groom took the piece of paper and stuffed it into his shirt pocket. "I think I can manage it. You left-handed or right?"

"Right."

"Okay." The man started hitching the scabbard to the right side of the saddle. "You want to take the price tags off this, Mister Cooper?"

"Yeah, tear 'em off and throw 'em away."

"Where'd you get all this gear?"

"Ordered it. Had it for some years now."

"Good stuff. That your bedroll?"

"Yeah, saddlebags and all this gear is mine. Got to put some stuff in here. How's it go in?"

"I'll do it for you. You reckon you'll need that much whiskey? How long you gonna be gone, you reckon?"

"Don't know rightly." Sherman Cooper laughed at his mimicry. "Don't rightly know."

Several minutes passed as the two men loaded the quiet animal with its burden. Finally Sherman sat in the saddle.

"Which way you reckon I oughta head?"

The young groom looked worried. "Mister Cooper, you've

done good on your riding lessons and you got a good horse here, but have you ever been out there by yourself?"

"Now, son, don't go to frettin'. I'm gonna be fine."

"Well, sir, this place is about seven hundred acres, and over beyond that ridge is federal land, so you can go quite a ways before dark. I believe I'd pull up about start of sunset to make camp. It takes a while."

"I know. I'm gonna be careful."

The young man stood back and said rather timidly, "Mister Cooper, I put that radio in your saddlebags. Now all you have to do is turn on the power, push the talk button, and tell us where you are if you get into trouble. We'll hear it right in the kitchen. If you see any kind of a fence, you'll know you've run out of free range, so to speak."

"I know the law, son."

"Yes sir, I'm sure you do. Well, enjoy yourself, and just give us a holler on that radio if you need anything."

Sherman Cooper stuck the bottle of whiskey between his legs and lit a cigarette. He made a clucking noise with his mouth and the mare stepped forward and started up the hill in a swaying lazy walk. Sherman looked briefly over his shoulder and said, "So long, partner."

"So long, Mister Cooper. Thank you."

The small man walked toward the house that sat on a rise above the barn. He walked into the kitchen and spoke to his wife. "This country is going crazy."

"Was that Mister Cooper?"

"Yeah, but he thinks he's John Wayne."

Phillip leaned forward with his hands under his chin. "In what way do you think he's changed? Maybe you're just getting to know him better."

Linda sat spraddle-legged in the stiff-backed chair and made a gesture of noncomprehension. "I don't know. I don't know. He just seems so moody." She lifted her eyes toward Phillip. There was fear in them. She spoke flatly. "Does Bill do drugs that you know of?"

Phillip sat upright and scratched his head. "Nothing hard, I don't think. Maybe a little grass now and then. What makes you ask?"

"I don't know anybody on coke. I'm suspicious, but I don't know that I could be sure. It worries me. Sometimes he just explodes with confidence, and at times he's afraid to open his mouth. Is that the way it works?"

"Sorry, I can't help you there."

Linda stood and rubbed her backside with the palms of her hands. "What'll I do with him if he's on something? He's not the most manageable person in the world. Lovable, but not manageable."

"Give 'im hell. He's slow getting a message, but he can be taught."

"I'm just getting used to being pregnant. Maybe it's just part of the syndrome. I'll ask my doctor about that. Now, wouldn't that . . ." Linda looked out the window. "I think Sally's back from shopping."

Phillip said, "Why don't you stay and eat a bite with us if Bill's not coming home for dinner? Sally's a good country cook."

Linda shrugged her shoulders. "I'm starved. I'll mix us a drink while Sally cooks. Okay?"

"Scotch neat for me."

"You got it."

Preacher Joseph Armes was unable to get his station wagon started. It had been past four o'clock when Linda Zephries had driven by. He stood outside his trailer home and looked up and down Route 31 for some signs of help. The people in the cars that came by were either locals who had become accustomed to the sight of the lean scraggly man in the dirty black suit and went their way, or they were tourists and curiosity seekers who slowed to stare at him. None stopped to inquire of his needs.

As if to say good-bye, the preacher walked a few steps from his trailer and turned to stare at it and the station wagon sitting dead and helpless alongside the road. He jerked his head away from the scene in finality and started walking toward his old homeplace. He marched in a boastful stride that denied the state of his health. It was a long, arduous journey traveling the hills, but walking through the countryside where he knew every tree, creek, and bush, he shortened the distance considerably.

He arrived at the site of his old homeplace and his parents' graves a little past dark. There was no moon, but his eyes had become accustomed to the dark. He sat between the graves in a patch of early spring grass, the dew seeping through to his fragile legs and buttocks.

He looked skyward and said, "Lord, I'm lost now. I am home, and I am absolutely lost. There's no way out of here. Not for me. Not from these hills. And have I served you in my prophecy? Have I made my life a journey for you? For your great honor? For thy glory?"

Joseph Armes reached into his coat pocket for a small bottle of whiskey that he carried. He took a long drink and came away from it gasping for breath. There was a burning sensation and then a quite cool flowing inside his chest and stomach. He leaned forward toward the grass and spewed forth a torrent of blood. He held his hands toward his face and felt the warm liquid flowing through his fingers. He recognized the problem. The abuse of diet and alcohol had eaten the lining from his stomach, and he was sick. He took a deep breath and felt the rumble inside again. The blood came from his mouth again and poured on the ground as if from a bucket. He knew it was blood now, for he could smell it. He rubbed his hands together for the warmth it offered from the chill of the evening. With each deep breath more blood came forth. He began to feel euphoric, glorious, wonderful. "Thank you, Lord Jesus," he said. "Thank you for a prophecy fulfilled."

He knew the fire would began to dance about him again as it had in his youth when he had first been called to his ministry, but he was too tired to watch, too happy to care, and too dead to notice.

CHAPTER FOURTEEN

BANG! AND BANG!

Wearing his black jumpsuit and driving the old black pickup, Gorman Weeds was all but invisible as he waited in the parking lot at Bill Zephries's apartment. He was getting impatient. The playboy lifestyle of Zephries, once a country boy, was breeding as much hatred in Weeds as the already festering wound of jealousy.

He had been trying to determine where the man went and when he was alone. He had thought the golf course would be a good place to do his deed, but there was always someone along. Gorman, who knew nothing about the game, wondered if people ever played golf alone. It was obvious that Zephries had decided not to go back to the old home place at Spring Hill. That would have been sweet revenge, thought Gorman Weeds — laying the son of a bitch to rest in his own dirt.

It was after the rush-hour traffic on West End Avenue in Nashville. Gorman had parked a block above Bill Zephries's apartment. He lounged in the pickup with a thermos of coffee. The thermos bottle was paint splattered and scarred from the many days it had spent on construction sites. There was a bottle of good Canadian whiskey in the glove compartment, but Weeds was not going to yield to the temptation of having a drink just yet. He waited with little patience and great anxiety for Zephries to come out of the apartment. His wife had left a little before four, but Bill Zephries was still inside.

It was after dark, some few minutes past eight, when Zephries finally came down the stairs from the apartment complex. He held a briefcase in his left hand and carried a lighted cigarette in his right. Gorman watched as his prey dug into his pockets for the keys to the Cadillac.

Gorman touched his hand to the ignition of the truck. He had to be ready. He had no idea which way Zephries might go. "Wherever the son of a bitch is going, there ain't nobody with him." Gorman was glad the woman was not along. He leaned over and checked to see that the Winchester, lever action, .30 calibre rifle was well back under the seat.

Bill Zephries's Cadillac pulled into traffic. Weeds started the truck, turned on the lights, and pulled into traffic two cars behind. They were headed to downtown Nashville. The Cadillac turned right on I-40, and Weeds slapped his hand on the seat. "The bastard is going toward Spring Hill." Maybe he was headed out to the old home place. At the intersection of I-65 and I-40, Zephries eased his Cadillac to the left lane, passed the I-65 exit, and continued on I-40 east. Weeds was directly behind now. Zephries was driving uncharacteristically slow. Weeds noted that they had hardly exceeded the fifty-five mile per hour limit.

As Weeds drove, he rubbed the back of his neck to get the catch out of it. Finally, yielding to the temptation and excited by the chase, he reached into the glove compartment, opened the bottle of whiskey, and took a long, sweet drink. One wouldn't hurt him. He was a good drinker. He could handle the stuff. Just one drink to keep him calmed down. Weeds savored the taste of the whiskey and kept his eyes glued on the tail lights of the Cadillac. They drove several miles east on I-40 toward Knoxville.

Gorman Weeds took one more small drink from the bottle of whiskey. He checked the rifle under the seat and turned on the radio. He muttered over the sound of the radio, talking to himself, "I hope you're not going to Virginia."

Bill Zephries searched his jacket pocket to find the little brown pouch, opened it, and retrieved the small packet of cocaine. He wet his finger and picked up a small amount of the drug, stuck it to his nose, and sniffed long and hard several times.

Linda and Phillip were alive with plans to restore the old house and grounds. "Well, the ten acres we've got is hilly," Phillip said.

Linda said, "Yes, but it's perfect, really. It's just the right amount of land for landscaping, and such beautiful things can be done when the lay of the land is irregular. This is going to be a showplace of the South. I'm going to do some research on the early history of the wood they used, the rock, the carpenters, and everything. I can dig it out, too. When I get started, I leave no stone, er, rock unturned." She laughed.

Sally Weeds stood at the sink washing dishes. Til had gone back to her friend's house. Linda and Sally had accepted one another for what the situation was. Linda bragged on the food and Sally accepted the compliments by saying it was plain old country cooking the way her mother had done it. Phillip enjoyed the food and the lively conversation and did not notice the sly glances the two women took at one another from time to time.

Linda looked at her watch. "I guess I'd better get on back to town before wild Bill comes in and finds me gone. I'll get these papers copied so we can all have a set. I want to get

together with all of you out here this weekend and cook something for us. We'll have our first summer outing at . . . Let's
come up with a name for this place. Like — oh, we'll think of
something antebellum. Maybe something will come out of my
research."

Linda stood and thanked Sally again. She noticed there
were only two cars in the drive and one of them was hers. She
said, "Sally, can I drop you off somewhere on my way out?"

Sally glanced at Phillip. He said, "Uh, no, that's okay, I'll
drop her off later."

Linda said, "Phillip, you should be neater here. You're leaving your underwear all over the bathroom. Good night."

Phillip followed her to the door. "Bachelors will be
bachelors."

It was ten-fifteen when Bill Zephries turned his Cadillac
off the interstate and drove some two miles out a state road
before pulling off into a wide meadow. Gorman Weeds had
kept on going until he was sure his tail lights were not visible
from the field. He had turned around and driven with the
lights out until he could see the outline of the Cadillac sitting
in the middle of the field. Weeds was parked on a small dirt
road surrounded by bushes and trees. He got out of the pickup
and took the rifle with him to a small knoll that overlooked the
field. He had had several drinks from the whiskey bottle. His
heart pounded as he sighted the rifle toward the Cadillac.
"What is the man doing out here in this damned place? I must
have stumbled into a whole pile of new shit here. I can't see
him. Why don't he get out of the car? What's he doin' just

sittin' there?" All these thoughts ran through Weeds's mind as he watched from the knoll.

At exactly ten-thirty another car entered the field and pulled up alongside Bill Zephries's car. There was an exchange of packages and some conversation that Weeds could not make out from his knoll some two hundred yards away. It was such a brief encounter that Weeds was taken by surprise when the two cars started pulling out of the field back toward the main road. Weeds ran back to his pickup. He started the engine and turned the pickup around in a small clearing and drove back to the main road. As he reached the road, he saw Zephries's Cadillac leaving the area at a breakneck speed. Weeds hit the gas pedal and followed the speeding Cadillac with his lights out. Suddenly another car came around a bend in the road and almost ran into a ditch when the driver apparently was startled by the black hulk of the pickup speeding along with its lights out. Weeds cursed the driver of the other car and caught sight of Zephries's car just as it made the entrance ramp to the interstate back toward Nashville. The Cadillac slowed to normal speed once on the interstate, and Weeds turned on his lights and followed several cars behind. Weeds was sweating and shaking from the chase, and so he had one more drink of the whiskey as he tried to formulate a plan in his mind as to what he could do with this startling information he had just become privy to.

Sherman Cooper lay by a smoldering campfire. He had hobbled his horse near water and grass, had read the instructions for unfolding and setting up his campfire grill, and had cooked wieners and beans for his supper.

Although he wasn't aware of it, Sherman was only a half mile away from a Ramada Inn where salesmen sat in the bar watching a boxing match on ESPN television. He had laid his bedroll out on the ground near the fire and was using his saddle for a pillow. A raccoon picked up the wiener he had thrown into the woods, stars twinkled overhead, a warm breeze rustled the leaves of the trees, and a jumbo jet roared somewhere in the distance taking Rosanna Zephries back to San Francisco.

Sherman Cooper unconsciously turned to his left side and slept better than he had in many years.

The old black pickup followed the Cadillac out I-65 South to the 96 exit at Franklin. There Bill Zephries had gone east on 96 and worked his way back into the hills. Weeds could not follow too closely, as the two cars were the only ones traveling on that stretch of road at that time.

Weeds rounded a curve to see the Cadillac turn left up a steep dirt road. He accelerated the pickup and drove on by. He now knew where Zephries was headed. There was a tobacco barn at the top of the hill on the dirt road and there the road ended. Zephries was on a dead end.

Once out of sight, Weeds pulled his pickup into a small clearing off the highway. He jumped from the truck and jerked the rifle from under the seat. He ran, crouching, back up the highway to the dirt road. He turned and ran to the top of the hill where he could see the Cadillac. The car was parked in front of the barn, the lights out. Weeds made himself comfortable behind a small bush. He could see the whole area.

Bill Zephries sat quietly in the car, watching behind him for any movement or vehicles. He saw none. He lit a cigarette and blew the smoke toward the floorboard. This was not as easy as he had first imagined. His heart pounded and he was sweating profusely.

Gorman Weeds watched as his man got from the Cadillac and approached the barn door. He laid the barrel in the crook of his arm and trained the sights on Zephries, who suddenly turned back to the car. There was a burst of bright light, and Gorman jerked back instantly, almost accidentally firing the rifle. Zephries had turned on the car's headlights to sort out the key to the locked barn door. Weeds again trained the rifle sights on the man at the barn, switched off the safety, and fired.

The scene was frozen for a moment. Bill Zephries whirled to face the sound of the gunfire. Weeds had missed. Zephries jerked the black handbag he was holding to the front of his chest, stared wide-eyed in the direction of the rifle, and started to run. A bullet crashed through the bag, hitting him in the chest. He hugged the bag tighter to his chest and stared down at it. He slowly lowered the bag and shouted, "Hey . . . I . . .What the hell . . . My God!"

Weeds fired again. The left side of Bill Zephries's head was blown away. All the light in the world entered his consciousness. He tried to remember something far away and long ago. He remembered everything at once. The motor that had moved his body for so many years would not respond. He wanted to block out the fascinating light. He could not lift his head from where it hung. "Mother . . . Linda, Phil, God . . ."

And he was dead, slumping forward into the dirt at the barn door.

Weeds was standing. He worked the lever of the rifle and fired into the scene where Bill Zephries lay dead. He was suddenly aware that the gun was not firing. He had used up the bullets. There was an awesome silence. Weeds walked quickly down the hill toward Zephries and the car, looking over his shoulder in panic. He trembled with an uncontrollable chill, but he kept the empty gun pointed toward his victim. When he reached the scene, he kicked at the body of Bill Zephries and screamed at him, "You son of a bitch, you . . ." He grabbed the black bag where it had fallen and started running back toward his pickup. He ran through briars, bushes, tripped over a fence. He didn't notice that the bag was leaking a fine white powder until he was near the truck. He quickly turned the bag hole-side-up and nursed it into the front seat. He grabbed a handful of McDonald's burger wrappers from the floor and stuffed them into the hole. He was beginning to get his wits about him.

As Weeds resisted the urge to speed back toward Nashville, he felt the gun slide toward him as he rounded a curve. He grabbed the barrel of the gun and entertained the notion to throw it onto the roadside but didn't. He felt the need to be back in the security of the only home he had — the unfurnished apartment.

Gorman pulled to the side of the road near a small bridge just long enough to throw his rifle into the Harpeth River. The old black pickup rattled and whined its way back to Nashville.

It was well toward one in the morning when a wild-eyed but safe Gorman Weeds made his way to the apartment where he had been staying. He carried a fresh bottle of whiskey and the now troublesome black bag with the cocaine in it.

Weeds sat on the floor of the unfurnished apartment and drank from the bottle of whiskey. He breathed deeply and looked wide-eyed at the wall. Speaking to no one, he said, "Well, see, I did it for Sally. See?"

Linda Zephries had laid down on the bed with her clothes on. She awakened at three A.M. and looked at the bedroom clock. She walked down the hallway into the kitchen and looked at the clock there. She rubbed the top of her head and looked at her wrist watch. She stood facing the kitchen phone for a moment. She reached for it and dialed the Old Zephries Place. She yawned as the phone rang in the old house. Phillip Zephries answered.

"Phillip, this is Linda. I hate to bother you at this time of night, but I'm worried about Bill."

"What time is it?"

"It's after three."

"I haven't heard from him here."

"He's never been out this late before."

"Well, you know, he gets with those tobacco guys, they play poker, drink a little, bullshit. I don't think I'd worry about him. He said he'd be out late, didn't he?"

"Yes, I guess he did. But all night?"

"He's okay. Get some sleep and try not to worry."

"Sorry I bothered you this late."

"That's okay. Just get some sleep."

Linda walked toward the bedroom removing her clothes. The TV was still on. She got into bed and watched Senator Gary Hart talking to some newsman. A few later minutes she was asleep.

At seven A.M. Phillip sat in the kitchen of the Old Zephries Place drinking coffee. Sally Weeds had not come down yet. Til was at the kitchen counter buttering toast. She looked out the window and said, "Phillip, they's a state police car out there."

"Where?"

"In the yard. Right here." She pointed out the window.

Phillip walked to the kitchen door, opened it, and stood looking at the car as two patrolmen emerged. One of the men held a clipboard. He glanced at the board and said, "Are you a relative of Bill Zephries?"

"Yes sir, his brother."

"Can you come out a minute?"

"Sure, what's wrong?" Phillip stepped outside, closing the door behind him.

Til watched from the kitchen window. Phillip took the clipboard from the man and stared at it. He handed it back and started talking excitedly to the man with the clipboard. The other patrolman bowed his head. Phillip started to his car, but the man grabbed his arm and talked to him while shrugging his shoulders. Phillip looked around in confusion, then turned his back to the two patrolmen and walked a short distance into the back yard. He turned and said something else. The two men shrugged. The man with the clipboard started reading from it, and Phillip was nodding his head.

Til ran to the kitchen door and flung it open. "What is it? What happened?"

Phillip turned and stared at her. "Bill, he . . ."

"What?"

"He's . . . he . . ."

Til threw her hands to her face, "Oh, my God!

Linda Zephries rolled over and grabbed the phone. She had slept fitfully. "Hello."

"Linda, this is Phillip."

"Where's Bill? Have you heard from him?"

"Linda, I want you to stay there. I'll be right over."

"Wait, where's Bill? Have you heard from Bill?"

"Listen, just stay there. I'll be right over."

"What are you coming over here for? Where's Bill? Answer me."

"He's been hurt. Listen, I'll be right over."

"Hurt? What's the matter with him?"

"I don't want to talk on the phone. I'll be over."

"Where is he? Is he in the hospital? What's wrong with him? What do you mean hurt? Phillip . . . what's wrong?" Linda's eye caught the TV screen. "Wait a minute, hold on . . . hold . . ." Ambulance attendants were wheeling a covered body from the front of a blood-splattered barn, a tobacco barn. The announcer was saying, "Chris, that's all we know at the time. The victim's relatives are being notified . . ."

Linda screamed into the phone, "Is that Bill on TV . . . is . . . what's happened?"

"Linda, calm down now."

"Calm down? I . . . Phillip, please, for God's sake, what happened? What hospital is he in? Tell me. I've got to go."

"He's not in the hospital. Stay there, please."

"He's not in the . . . my God, get him to a hospital. Are you crazy? Get him in there."

"Linda . . ."

Linda Zephries was suddenly very quiet. She tried to say the words, "He's . . . he, my God, he's your brother, Phillip. He's my husband. Do you know what you're trying to say? My God, Phillip, you can't say that. Can you say that? Phillip?"

"I'm sorry, Linda, we . . . He's dead." Linda jerked the phone from the outlet and flung it across the room. She sat quietly staring at a cereal commercial. A young man was smiling over the top of a large spoon and a white bowl. Linda Zephries started to sob uncontrollably.

Two policemen stood outside Linda's apartment. One turned to the other. "From what I can hear, she already knows. You want to go in?"

"I hate this kind of detail."

"Me too. Make a note that she already knew."

The two men left the sounds of sobbing and walked downstairs. One said, "Man, when they say Cadillac of drugs, they're talking Cadillac of drugs with coke. This is a ritzy apartment complex."

"Word is they left a shitpot of it on the ground out there."

"Messy."

"You know what's gonna happen? Some hog is gonna come sniffing around out there on that farm, and in five minutes he's gonna think he's a thoroughbred racehorse."

The two men laughed.

A long, dark Lincoln Continental sped down I-65 north from Spring Hill to the apartment where Gorman Weeds lay sleeping. The small, dark man said, "It has to be him. It wasn't a system hit. It had to be an accidental deal."

The tall, pale man at the wheel nodded his head. "We'll see."

"Here's how I see it. Weeds just caught the guy who was into his pussy in a nice dark place and wasted him."

The pale man said, "We'll see."

"The people we talked to in Spring Hill said—"

"We'll see."

"I'm just telling you we don't do business that way. It was a coincidence. Who would leave all that coke spilled all over a cow pasture? He couldn't know what was in the bag or that it had a hole in it as big as a cow's ass."

"We'll see."

The pale man looked to his right. "Is that the place?"

The dark man checked some notes. "Yeah, down that construction road. Number 23-B."

The two men stepped from the long black car and hit the steps running. The pale man said, "Watch my back."

"Got it."

The two men stepped briskly down the hallway. They stopped at 23-B, and the dark man motioned for the pale man to step out of the way. He raised his foot and kicked.

Gorman Weeds sat upright at the sound of the loud crash and the splintering wood. He shook his head and rubbed his eyes. "Hey? . . . uh, what the hell . . ."

The pale man stood facing the startled Gorman. "You Weeds?" He motioned the dark man to a black bag lying against the wall. "Is that it?"

The dark man said, "Think so. Yeah, this is it."

Gorman Weeds looked into the barrel of a pistol with a funny looking attachment on the front. "You guys know me?" He looked at the pale man. "Hey, I know you. I see you—"

There were two loud thumping noises. Gorman looked sadly at the pale man, then turned and looked pleadingly at the dark man. Gorman's feelings were hurt. He look down at his chest and wiped something wet off his shirt. He felt the way he had felt when his father had hit him with a piece of stove-wood when he was a child. He started to cry. "Hey, fellahs, I mean . . . you didn't have . . . What is . . ."

Gorman heard a door closing. They had turned out the lights. "Hey, you turned out . . ."

Gorman heard a faint voice from somewhere. "Don't cry, honey, don't give him the satisfaction. Don't cry."

Gorman sniffed, "I know, Mama, but they turned out . . ."

George Atworth had just gotten off the plane and checked into his hotel. He drew the curtains back from the window of his room in the Sheraton in Nashville. He stood looking at the dreary countryside and thought, "Now what honky mother-fucker ever thought of putting the world's greatest automobile plant here in this grab-ass boondock? I mean, what a waste. What jive-ass thought of it in the first place? Man, we're talk-ing three billion train-ridin' dollars dumped into a white-trash ghetto."

The young black man suddenly laughed at his dialect. Here he was with an MG parked in some lonely garage in Detroit, a wardrobe of clothes that would rival Bryant Gumbel, a delicious lady waiting for him to call, and he was talking like a street-wise dude from the war zones of Detroit.

George Atworth dusted a speck from his sportcoat and looked around the room in despair. It had been the best of all possible worlds to be a half-breed in Detroit, a half-breed city. A good town where people had come as close to integration as America would ever get. He resented his mother and his dead father. They had not made the best of it. They had not been able to see the potential out there. They had lacked vision. He had been glad when his mother had succeeded in real estate because that had taken her off his back and kept her busy. She had hardly known what to say to him when she had made her life's work a war with Amanda Zephries. He had argued with her that the quest was not worth the prize, that her sons would not know her or care about her. He thought it an impossible dream to get even with an old woman with one foot in the grave, impossible to relive a life that had passed by.

The quest had caused an even wider rift in their relationship, and he felt helpless in that regard.

And yet, when he had been offered the assignment to come to Spring Hill, he had jumped at the chance to see for himself. His half-brothers, the town, his mother's homeplace, and the sad irony in all of it.

And when he had seen it, he was ready to leave, to forget, to get on with his life, and to stand in a shower in his own apartment in Detroit and let the waters of the northern rivers wash his sins and his memories away.

Yet he felt obligated, through some deep sense of tradition, to go to the funeral of his half-brother. It would be over in a few hours, and he could catch a plane back home. On thinking it over, he doubted that he would ever see his mother again after this. She had given him up for this wild and senseless war of blood, and he had lost her before it even started.

CHAPTER FIFTEEN

RESOLUTION

Phillip Zephries drove north toward I-65 and the I-24 exit that would take him to St. Louis. The good-byes had all been said. The bewildering feeling that had come over all of them after the funeral seemed to draw them all together—to talk, to find some answers, to right some wrongs and plan for the future. But it was all too selfish. Each of them really wanted to be alone and sort out feelings. Maybe there would be a gathering later. Someday.

Sally Weeds sat in the front seat of the car with Phillip. She twisted her hands in her lap and looked anxiously down the road. "Phillip, do you think we're doing the right thing? I've never been out of Tennessee. What will they think of me in St. Louis?"

Phillip looked straight ahead. "It doesn't matter what they think of you. It's just another town."

Sally was still dressed in the black dress she had worn to Gorman's funeral. Her eyes were red and she trembled in the bright sunshine. She said, "Phillip, I'm sorry I couldn't go to Bill's funeral. I couldn't stand two in one day, and Gorman's mama was so broke up, I couldn't leave her."

Phillip said, "It's okay. I understand."

She would occasionally sigh deeply and wipe tears from her eyes. She turned and looked at the handsome young man at the wheel. "Phillip, promise me something. If you get tired of me in St. Louis, you just send me right on back to Spring Hill."

Phillip ignored the statement. "You know something? It's strange how things turn out. Now there's Linda back there at the Old Zephries Place bringing twins into the world. Said she wanted to raise them there. There's Til, been there for over thirty years—she wants to stay and help raise the children. And these will be Saturn's children, won't they? In a strange way, it all comes back to that. As if one generation had moved away with the old brush and weeds and a new generation set in place as if it were all part of a plan."

Widow Weeds lay on the bed in the little house where she lived. Her friend Thelma came into the room and said, "They're all gone now, so I'm putting the food away. You sure you can't eat a little something?"

The weary old woman sat upright on the bed and put her feet on the floor. She tucked her dress between her legs and clamped her knees together. She leaned her head toward her knees and spoke quietly. "Thank you, Thelma. I don't reckon I could. Did Wilma take some of that pie with her? She loves that pecan pie, and we couldn't eat it all. You know, Gorman loved pecan pie. He could eat two or three pieces and drink a half a gallon of milk if I'd let him. Did she take some with her?"

"She took a bite. Said you might have more folks coming in."

Widow Weeds lifted her head and looked around the room. "What time is it? It must be awful late."

"It's only about three-thirty."

"In the evening?"

"Yes."

"Why wouldn't that man let me stay out there a while? Is he crazy or somethin'? I need to stay out there with Gorman."

"There was nothing you could do."

Widow Weeds stomped both feet on the floor. "I wish people would stop saying there's nothin' I can do. I can do somethin'. I could stay out there with Gorman a while." The woman looked around the room. "What time is it?"

"About three-thirty."

"Where's them police?"

"They've been gone since yesterday."

"Did they find out who done it?"

"No. You sure you can't eat a bite?"

"No. Did Wilma take some of that pecan pie?"

"Yes."

"Good. You know what them police said? Said Gorman was puttin' cheap stuff on the job and was selling the good stuff to crooks. Said he was mixed up with somebody. Gorman never stole a thing in his life. Did you ever hear the beat?"

"No. It was a nasty thing for them to say."

"Did you eat some of that pie?"

"Yes. Would you like a little piece with a glass of milk?"

"I might try a little bite. Reckon I oughta keep something on my stomach."

"I'll get it for you."

Thelma went into the kitchen and came back with a piece of pecan pie on a small plate and held a glass of milk. Widow Weeds was down on her knees looking under the bed. "His gun ain't here. He took it with him. He always left it under here when he didn't use it. Do you see any gun under here?"

Thelma set the milk and pie on a small table, lay down on the floor, and looked under the bed. "Nothing under there."

The two women got to their feet. Widow Weeds swayed unsteadily. "He woulda shot back. They got his gun somewheres. They oughta find that gun. That'd tell who killed him."

"Honey, sit down and eat this pie and drink some milk. You need to keep your strength up."

"Did Wilma take some of this pie? She just loves pecan pie."

Til sat in a chair by the small kitchen table. Linda Zephries stood with her stomach resting against the kitchen counter and looked through the window at the fading afternoon. Everyone had gone home.

"Til?"

"Uh huh."

"I want you to go with some men and get my things out of that apartment. I can't bear to go back there again. Just get my things."

"You don't have to go back there if you don't want to."

There was more silence in what had been a very silent afternoon.

Linda said, "Thank you for agreeing to stay on here."

"Ain't got no place else to go. I'se been here, and I am here. Dat's all I know."

Linda stood silent. Til said, "Gotta bring them azalea bushes back out here 'fore dey die, 'fore dey wilt away, I mean."

Linda Zephries lit a cigarette. Til said, "I thought you gonna quit them things."

"I am, I am."

"The police through talkin' to you?"

"I hope so."

"Dey jes tryin' to help."

"They said it was organized crime. We may never know."

"It ain't gonna make no difference to dem babies. Dat's what you gotta worry 'bout now."

Linda stood back and rubbed her stomach. "Oh, Til, what would I do without you?"

"You ain't gonna do nothin' 'thout me. Dat's what."

Linda Zephries wiped a tear from her cheek and looked through the window toward the far hills. "Til, we're going to restore this place. I want to restore this grand old furniture. We'll have hundreds of azalea bushes. We're going to paint, scrape, nail, hammer, weed, dig, sweat, cry, break our backs, until this is the showplace of the South. Our babies are going to grow up in the midst of history. Not old history, but recent history. I want them to know everything that happened. I don't want to hide anything the way Rosanna did. I want it all out in the open. I want them to learn to love this place. I think I'll call it Jupiter, God of light, of the sky and weather, and of the state and its welfare and its laws. Do you like that?"

Til bowed her head and she mumbled, "It's bad luck to make plans on a funeral day."

"Who told you that?"

"It ain't nothin' nobody told me. It's a fact."